# CIVIL RIGHTS:
*Rhetoric or Reality?*

*Previously Published Books*

# CIVIL RIGHTS:
## *Rhetoric or Reality?*

## By Thomas Sowell

QUILL   WILLIAM MORROW
NEW YORK

Library of Congress Cataloging-in-Publication Data

Sowell, Thomas, 1930–
Civil rights.

Includes bibliographical references and index.
1. Civil rights—United States.   2. Affirmative
action programs—United States.   3. Ethnic groups.
4. United States—Race relations.   I. Title.
JC599.U5S599   1985      323.1'73      85-19131
ISBN 0-688-06269-5 (pbk.)

Printed in the United States of America

First Quill Edition

1 2 3 4 5 6 7 8 9 10

BOOK DESIGN BY PATRICE FODERO

To E. Franklin Frazier,
who put truth above popularity

# PREFACE

Some books are written for the pleasure or the zest of it. Other books are written as a painful duty, because there is something that needs to be said—and because other people have better sense than to say it. It has not been a pleasure to write this book but a necessity. Nothing is more certain than its distortion. Yet the growing polarization of the races, the stagnation and retrogression of the truly disadvantaged, and the embittered atmosphere surrounding the evolution of "civil rights," in the courts especially, leave no real alternative to an open and frank reconsideration of what has been done, and is being done, in the name of those two words.

Civil rights are among the most honored achievements of Western civilization. In the United States, civil rights for all people has been a goal for which an uphill fight has been waged, literally for centuries, at great human cost—including the lives of many who dared to stand up for what was right, even when it would have been far more expedient to look the other way. The Supreme Court decision against racial segregation in May 1954 was a landmark victory over some of the ugliest forces buried in American history. Yet the more honored and stirring any concept is, the more certain it is to be misused for the benefit of special interests.

7

The Bible was used to justify slavery. "Civil rights" has come to mean many very different things—including some meanings that would be both foreign and repugnant to many of those whose struggles and sacrifices made civil rights possible.

Thirty years after the historic decision in *Brown* v. *Board of Education* is an appropriate time to reconsider where we have come and where we are going. It is also twenty years after the Civil Rights Act of 1964, a legislative landmark comparable to the judicial breakthrough of a decade earlier. How much of the promise of these judicial and legislative events has been fulfilled? How much has it been perverted? How well has the social vision behind the civil rights movement been understood—or even questioned? These are the issues addressed in the pages that follow.

*Hoover Institution*
February 10, 1983

# ACKNOWLEDGMENTS

No man is an island. Our debts to others stretch far back into the mists of time. Special acknowledgments are due, however, to the Hoover Institution, which allows me the time and the freedom from teaching and administrative chores to explore such issues as I choose at the pace that I choose. This book, for example, began as an attempt to write an article, which simply grew beyond its bounds. A debt of gratitude is also due the Manhattan Institute, which has repeatedly done a superb job in organizing forums in which my ideas and books were made known to the media and the intellectual community, and which has disseminated these proceedings widely throughout the country. These gatherings have been important to me in gauging the issues and approaches that give others the most difficulty, and I have tried to keep these in mind in the presentation in this book. I wish also to express my appreciation to the *Wayne Law Review* and to *Policy Review*, both of which permitted me to copyright articles I wrote for them, parts of which reappear in this book. The most special debt, however, is due to my wife, who has not only discussed and criticized the ideas in this and other books, but who has also provided much of the personal setting in which both work and happiness can flourish.

# CONTENTS

## CHAPTER ONE

# THE CIVIL RIGHTS VISION

May 17, 1954 was a momentous day in the history of the United States, and perhaps of the world. Something happened that afternoon that was all too rare in human history. A great nation voluntarily acknowledged and repudiated its own oppression of part of its own people. The Supreme Court decision that day was announced in an atmosphere of high drama, and some observers said that one of the black-robed Justices sat on the great bench with tears in his eyes.

*Brown* v. *Board of Education* was clearly much more than another legal case to go into the long dusty rows of volumes of court decisions. It represented a vision of man and of the world that touched many hearts across the land and around the world. The anger and rancor it immediately provoked also testified to its importance. In a larger historic context, that such an issue should reach the highest court in the land was itself remarkable. In how many places and in how many eras could an ordinary person from a despised race challenge the duly constituted authorities, force them to publicly defend their decisions, retreat, and finally capitulate?

*Brown* v. *Board of Education* may have been intended to close the door on an ugly chapter in American history, going back to slavery and including both petty and gross bigotry, blatant discrimination, and violence and terror extending all the way to brutal and sadistic lynchings. Yet it also opened a door to political, constitutional, and human crises. It was not simply a decision but the beginning of a revolution that has not yet run its course, but which has already shown the classic symptoms of a revolution taking a very different path from that envisioned by those who set it in motion.

The civil rights revolution of the past generation has had wide ramifications among a growing variety of groups, and has changed not only the political landscape and social history of the United States, but has also altered the very concept of constitutional law and the role of courts.

Behind the many visible changes has been a change in the way the world is visualized. The civil rights vision is not only a moral vision of the way the world *should* be in the future, but also a cause-and-effect vision of the way the world *is* today. This cause-and-effect vision of the way the world works is central to understanding the particular direction of thrust of the civil rights revolution, its achievements, its disappointments, and its sharp changes in meaning that have split its supporters and confounded its critics.

It is far from incidental that the civil rights movement began among black Americans. The basic vision of what was wrong, and of what social effects would follow from what institutional changes, bore the clear imprint of the history of blacks in the United States, though the general principles arrived at were later applied successively to very different groups in American society—to women and the aged, for example, as well as to such disparate racial and ethnic groups as Asians, Hispanics, and American Indians. It is now estimated that 70 percent of the American population is entitled to preferential treatment under "affirmative action."[1] The civil rights vision has even been extended

14

internationally to the plight of the Third World and to racial policies in other nations, such as South Africa.

Ironically, the civil rights revolution began by emphasizing precisely what was unique about the history of black Americans—slavery, Jim Crow laws, and some of the most virulent racism ever seen anywhere. But upon that very uniqueness, *general* principles of morality and causation were established. These principles constitute the civil rights vision of the world. The extent to which that vision corresponds to reality is crucial for understanding both the successes and failures of the civil rights revolution thus far, and for assessing its future prospects and dangers.

# SPECIAL CASES AND GENERAL PRINCIPLES

Because civil rights laws and civil rights concepts are applied generally—to both racial and non-racial groups—their *general* validity must be examined. The special case of blacks can then be examined precisely as a special case.

One of the most central—and most controversial—premises of the civil rights vision is that statistical disparities in incomes, occupations, education, etc., represent moral inequities, and are caused by "society." Historically, it was easy to show, for example, that segregated white schools had had several times as much money spent per pupil as in segregated black schools and that this translated into large disparities in physical plant, teacher qualifications, and other indices of educational input. Large differences in educational output, such as test scores, seemed readily attributable to these input differences. How well this model applied to other statistical disparities for other groups is another question entirely. Moreover, even for blacks, the causal link has been established by immediate

15

plausibility rather than by systematic verification of an hypothesis.

Another central premise of the civil rights vision is that belief in innate inferiority explains policies and practices of differential treatment, whether expressed in overt hostility or in institutional policies or individual decisions that result in statistical disparities. Moral defenses or causal explanations of these statistical differences in any other terms tend themselves to fall under suspicion or denunciation as racism, sexism, etc. Again, the question must be raised as to the general validity of these premises, as well as the separate question of their applicability to the special case of blacks.

A third major premise of the civil rights vision is that political activity is the key to improving the lot of those on the short end of differences in income, "representation" in desirable occupations or institutions, or otherwise disadvantaged. Once more, it is possible to cite such things as dramatic increases in the number of black elected officials after passage of the civil rights legislation of the 1960s. But once again, the general validity of the premise for the wide variety of groups covered by civil rights policies must be examined as a separate issue. And once again, even the special case of blacks must be systematically analyzed.

## Statistical Disparities

Several unspoken assumptions underlie the principle that statistical disparities imply discrimination. The first, and apparently most obvious, is that discrimination leads to adverse effects on the observable achievements of those who are discriminated against, as compared to the discriminators or to society in general. The second assumption is that the converse of this is equally true—that statistical differences signal, imply and/or measure discrimination. This assumption depends upon a third un-spoken premise—that large statistical differences between groups do not usually arise and persist without discrimination. For if they do, then discrimination takes its place as only one cause among many—and inferences from statistical disparities lose their validity as evidence. Discrimination may still exist and be harmful, but the convenient statistical barometer would be lost. Even a disease that is fatal 100 percent of the time provides no automatic explanation of death if there are many other fatal diseases, along with accidents, murder, and suicide. These are the inherent pitfalls of inductive reasoning. Even if $A$ is known to cause $Z$, we still cannot infer $A$ whenever we find $Z$, if $B$, $C$, $D$, etc., also cause $Z$.

How important are other factors besides discrimination in producing vast statistical disparities? The civil rights vision is one of a more or less random statistical distribution of results (income, "representation," test scores, etc.) in the absence of discrimination of one sort or another. Alternative visions are also conceivable, but the crucial question here is not plausibility but how to test any given vision against observable factual evidence.

There are many decisions wholly within the discretion of those concerned, where discrimination by others is not a factor—the choice of television programs to watch, opinions to express to poll takers, or the age at which to marry, for example. All these show pronounced patterns that differ from group to group—not a random distribution.

A whole industry exists to determine the statistical profile of people who view given television programs, for the differences between the demographic and economic characteristics of the respective audiences for sports events, "soap operas," cartoon programs, news features, etc., are worth millions of dollars to advertisers and networks. Public opinion polls show similarly wide disparities on many issues by income, education, sex, age, and religion. Marital patterns also differ widely from one group to another. For example, half of all Mexican American wives were married in their teens while only 10 percent of Japanese American wives were married that young.[2]

People do not move randomly, either within a nation or between nations. The great movement of nineteenth century European immigrants to the United States was largely a movement of young adults.[3] So was the great migration of blacks out of the South, beginning in the early twentieth century.[4] Of the Chinese immigrants to the United States before the First World War, 60 percent came from only one of 98 districts in one province in southern China.[5] Among Japanese immigrants to the United States in 1935, more than 90 percent of those from Okinawa went to Hawaii, while a majority of those from the Hiroshima area went to the mainland of the United States.[6] At the same time, Japanese emigrants from the area around Nagasaki went primarily to China and southeast Asia.[7] In post-World War II Japan, 70 percent of the emigrants from the Hidaka district settled in Canada, and of these, 90 percent from one village settled in one area of Canada.[8] Among German emigrants in the early nineteenth century, a majority went to South America, but from the 1830s to the end of the century, 90 percent went to the United States.[9] Among those Germans who emigrated to Chile in the mid-nineteenth century, most came from just one city, Hamburg.[10] Among the Jews scattered through the many countries of Latin America today, nearly half live in just one city, Buenos Aires.[11]

The sex composition of immigrants has also shown great disparities, both within groups and between groups. In the late nineteenth and early twentieth centuries, about 80 percent of all emigrants from Italy were male.[12] Among Chinese and Japanese immigrants to the United States during the same era, the men outnumbered the women by more than twenty-to-one,[13] and there were virtually no children. But among the Irish immigrants to the United States, the sex ratio was roughly even, and in some decades females outnumbered males.[14]

Statistical disparities extend into every aspect of human life. In major league baseball, for example, black players have hit home runs with significantly greater frequency than white players (in proportion to their respective times at bat) and with nearly twice the frequency of Latin players.[15] Of the five highest totals of home runs in a lifetime, three are by black players. But of the ten highest slugging averages ever achieved in a season, seven are by players of German ancestry—indeed, just two players, Babe Ruth and Lou Gehrig. Of the five times that someone has stolen 100 or more bases in a season, all were by black players.

In the toy industry, firms do not spend their annual television advertising budgets evenly—that is, 25 percent in each quarter of the year. Some of the best known toy manufacturers spend upwards of three-quarters or four-fifths of their annual television advertising budget in the last quarter.[16]

In short, statistical disparities are commonplace among human beings. Many historical and cultural reasons underlie the peculiar patterns observed. But the even "representation" of groups chosen as a baseline for measuring discrimination is a myth rather than an established fact. It is significant that those who have assumed that baseline have seldom, if ever, been challenged to produce evidence.

The civil rights vision focuses on groups *adversely* affected in statistical disparities. Here the relationship between discrimination and economic, educational, and other disadvantages is taken as virtually axiomatic. But if this apparently obvious proposition is taken as an hypothesis to be tested, rather than an axiom to be accepted, a very different picture emerges. Groups with a demonstrable history of being discriminated against have, in many countries and in many periods of history, had higher incomes, better educational performance, and more "representation" in high-level positions than those doing the discriminating.

Throughout southeast Asia, for several centuries, the Chinese minority has been—and continues to be—the target of explicit, legalized discrimination in various occupations, in admission to institutions of higher learning, and suffers bans and restrictions on land ownership and places of residence. Nowhere in Malaysia, Indonesia, Vietnam, Thailand, or the Philippines have the Chinese ever experienced equal opportunity. Yet in all these countries the Chinese minority—about 5 percent of the population of southeast Asia—owns a majority of the nation's total investments in key industries. By the middle of the twentieth century, the Chinese owned 75 percent of the rice mills in the Philippines, and between 80 and 90 percent of the rice mills in Thailand.[17] They conducted more than 70 percent of the retail trade in Thailand, Vietnam, Indonesia, Cambodia, the Philippines, and Malaysia.[18] In Malaysia, where the anti-Chinese discrimination is written into the Constitution, is embodied in preferential quotas for Malays in government and private industry alike, and extends to admissions and scholarships at the universities, the average Chinese continues to earn twice the income of the average Malay.[19]

Nor are the Chinese minorities in southeast Asia unique. Much the same story could be told of the Jews in many countries around the world and in many periods of history.[20] A similar pattern could also be found among East Indians in Africa, southeast Asia and parts of the western hemisphere, or among Armenians in the Middle East, Africa, and the United States. Italian immigrants to Argentina in the late nineteenth and early twentieth centuries also encountered discrimination, but nevertheless rose from poverty to affluence, surpassing the Argentine majority. Around the turn of the century, when Italians were 14 percent of the Argentine population, they owned more than twice as many food and drinking establishments in Buenos Aires as the native Argentines. They also owned more than three times as many shoe stores and more than ten times as many barbershops.[21] Japanese immigrants to the United States also encountered persistent and escalating discrimination, culminating in their mass internment during World War II, but by 1959 they had about equaled the income of whites and by 1969 Japanese American families were earning nearly one-third higher incomes than the average American family.[22]

In short, two key assumptions behind the civil rights vision do not stand up as general principles. The first is that discrimination leads to poverty and other adverse social consequences, and the second is the converse—that adverse statistical disparities imply discrimination. How well these assumptions hold up in the special case of American Negroes is a separate question to be dealt with in Chapter 4.

## Innate Inferiority

The civil rights vision tends to dichotomize the spectrum of possible reasons for group differences into (1) discrimination and (2) innate inferiority. Rejecting the latter, they are left with the former. Moreover, others who reject the former are regarded as believing the latter. Finally, institutional practices that either differentiate explicitly (as between men and women, for example) or have differential impact (test scores of blacks vs. whites) are attributed to their proponents' overt or tacit belief in innate inferiority.

Historically, the innate inferiority doctrine has of course been most prominent in issues revolving around blacks,

21

even though the reasoning has been extended to other contexts. But the more general question is the extent to which it explains intergroup hostility, discrimination, oppression, and violence.

It is difficult to know in what units to measure degrees of hostility or hatred, but overt violence, and especially lethal violence, leave factual records. For example, as many as 161 blacks have been lynched in one year in the United States.[23] How does this compare, historically, with violence against groups who were *not* widely viewed as innately inferior?

Many of the groups most subject to violence have not been generally viewed as innately inferior. Indeed, many have been hated precisely because of superior performances as economic competitors. That has been especially true of "middleman minorities" such as the Chinese in southeast Asia, and the Jews, East Indians, and Armenians in a number of countries around the world. All have been subjected to mass expulsions by various governments and to mass violence by the surrounding populace, sometimes aided and abetted by government. The number of Chinese killed within a few days, at various times in the history of southeast Asia, has on a number of occasions exceeded all the blacks ever lynched in the history of the United States.[24] Similarly with the massive slaughter of the Armenians in Turkey in the early twentieth century, and numerous massacres of Jews in Europe over the centuries, culminating in the Nazi Holocaust.

Even the enslavement of blacks was not the result of a doctrine of innate inferiority. On the contrary, this doctrine developed as a rationalization of slavery already in existence and under fire from both moral and political critics. Moreover, innate inferiority was not even the first rationalization used. Religious rationalizations—enslaving "heathens" for their own spiritual good—were first used and then abandoned as more slaves became Christians, and the innate inferiority doctrine was then substituted. This pattern was common both to the United States and to South Africa, though it was East Indians who were enslaved by South African whites. Moreover, in Brazil, the largest importer of slaves into the western hemisphere, the innate inferiority doctrine was rarely used.[25]

In short, belief in the innate inferiority doctrine has been neither necessary nor sufficient to explain intergroup hostility, oppression, violence, or enslavement.

Ironically, the innate inferiority doctrine and the opposite "equal representation" doctrine proceed on the same intellectual premise—that one can go from innate ability to observed result without major concern for intervening cultural factors. Unexplained residual differences between groups, after controlling for such gross differences as education or parental income, are attributed by one vision to discrimination and by the other to genetics. (As one who has opposed both doctrines,[26] it is particularly striking to me that so few have noticed their essential similarity of reasoning.)

Just how far the civil rights vision can take this line of reasoning was demonstrated by Supreme Court Justices in the *Bakke* and *Weber* cases. Alan Bakke could not have outperformed minority candidates applying to the same medical school if it were not for prior discrimination against these minority candidates, according to four of the Justices.[27] Similarly, Brian Weber would not have been able to compete successfully with black workers applying for the same training program, for "any lack of skill" on the black workers' part resulted from "purposeful discrimination in the past."[28] There are apparently no other reasons for differences in skill or capability other than discrimination, which is illegal, or innate inferiority, which is rejected. Or so it appears in the civil rights vision.

The extension of this kind of reasoning to sex differences is particularly arbitrary. In many instances, the desire to separate men from women is based on the premise that both sexes behave differently when together than when apart—regardless of whether either performs better or worse than the other. All-male and all-female schools and colleges, for example, may be established on the premise that either can be educated more effectively without the distracting or inhibiting presence of the other. The extent to which this is true, and for what kinds of students, is a separate question. The point here is simply that its basis has nothing to do with innate inferiority. Likewise, employers drawing upon a largely male labor pool may prefer an *all*-male work force, rather than one in which one or two women become the focus of male attentions to the detriment of the work, even if the women themselves are fully as productive as the men. Whatever the empirical validity or social policy implications of such employer preferences, innate inferiority is neither necessary nor sufficient to explain them.

Police departments, fire departments, the military and other organizations, where life-and-death decisions must be made, often seek a level of discipline, morale, and dedication to organizational purposes that they do not want compromised by powerful emotional attachments that can develop and cut across these organizational objectives. For this reason, such organizations may be particularly resistant to the introduction of women, as well as homosexuals, or even to members of the same family serving on active duty side by side. Again, inferiority doctrines are neither necessary nor sufficient to explain their position.

Potential hostility, as well as affinity, is among the reasons for separating various groups. Nineteenth-century American employers discovered to their loss that having Irish Protestants and Irish Catholics working together and living together on such projects as building railroads and digging canals was an open invitation to violence.[29] Later, they discovered the same to be true when the work gangs included Italians from different parts of Italy.[30] Some drinking establishments in nineteenth-century England became the exclusive domain of Irish immigrants from a given county in Ireland, because of the dangers of violence even among Irish Catholics from different counties.[31] Nor is violence necessary to cause segregation, especially in social activities. In late nineteenth-century Prague, for example, Czechs and Germans had separate pubs.[32]

In the United States, black-white separation has historically also included severe discrimination against blacks. "Separate but equal" was a transparent legal fiction. Yet discrimination cannot be *generalized* from separation. Even in the special case of blacks, the discrimination that accompanied segregation was much more prevalent and more severe in some situations than in others. At this point, however, the issue is simply whether separation necessarily implies discrimination and an innate inferiority doctrine—as general principles. It does not, either in logic or experience.

Those who dichotomize the reasons for intergroup differences into discrimination and innate inferiority not only ignore many other specific reasons, but more generally proceed as if "society" shapes groups themselves, in addition to making biased decisions about them. A series of landmark civil rights cases have declared illegal various mental tests, voting qualifications, and other standards—even when applied impartially—on the ground that society itself has made it much more difficult for some groups to acquire the skills in question, or even to stay out of jail, where employers have refused to hire people with a criminal record.[33]

Once again, the special case of blacks must be distinguished from the general principles of the civil rights vision, as it applies to 70 percent of the population. To what extent has "society" shaped groups—and in what sense? If the whole range of causal factors are dichotomized into heredity and environment, then all who are not racists or sexists are led by the logic of the argument to the view, expressed long ago by Locke, that people enter the world with their minds as blank pages on which society writes what it will. But the momentous consequences of this vision require it to be examined more closely.

What is "environment"? If it consists only of immediate surrounding circumstances, then the causal and moral responsibilities of a given society are quite different from what they would be if environment includes behavior patterns that go back for centuries, that originated in other countries thousands of miles away, and that follow each group wherever it settles around the world. In this latter case, it would be strange indeed if merely crossing the political boundaries of the United States were to magically homogenize groups that are so different everywhere else. Blacks may have lost much of their African culture in the centuries of slavery, but the question is whether that unique history provides a general principle.

It is not a foregone conclusion but an empirical question whether the Irish, the Chinese, the Germans, etc., in various lands are more like the other peoples of those lands or more like the people in their respective countries of origins and their kinsmen elsewhere around the globe.

A number of studies over the years have shown Irish Americans to have higher rates of alcohol consumption than Americans as a whole, and correspondingly higher rates of alcohol-related diseases. Nor are these differences small. For example, one study found the rate of alcoholic psychosis among Irish Americans to be 5 times that among Italian Americans and 50 times that among Jewish Americans.[34] Those who see society as the cause of such phenomena would be hard pressed to find in the history of Irish Americans sufficient traumas *not suffered by Jewish and Italian Americans as well* to explain such differences. Moreover, high rates of alcohol consumption in Ireland go back for centuries. Today Ireland spends a higher percentage of its income on alcohol than any other nation in Europe.[35] People of Irish ancestry are only 7 percent of the population of Birmingham, England, but they constitute 60 percent of those arrested for drunkenness.[36] By contrast, both the Jewish and Italian cultures in Europe have historically featured the drinking of wine—not hard liquor, as in Ireland—and both cultures have made drunkenness taboo. These patterns existed before American society existed.

The Chinese have established reputations for working hard and long, in countries around the world, and for not being stopped by the stigma of "menial" work. In nineteenth-century Siam, the rickshaws were virtually all pulled by Chinese, for the Siamese would not stoop to such work.[37] The Chinese were also known as the first to get up in the morning in Bangkok,[38] and throughout southeast Asia they worked incredibly long hours often under exhausting conditions.[39] They did most of the hard industrial work and mining in Malaya.[40] They were imported *en masse* into South Africa for similar work, in the early twentieth century, and were later sent home after clamor by white workers who could not compete with them.[41] In the United States, Chinese immigrants were used in many arduous jobs—including building railroad tracks through the rugged Sierra mountains, a task which most white workers either abandoned shortly after being hired or else refused to do at the outset, once they were at the site and saw what was expected of them.[42]

In intellectual as well as manual work, the Chinese have been disproportionately represented in the difficult and demanding fields such as mathematics, science, and technology. In Malaysia, where Malay college students outnumber the Chinese three-to-one in liberal arts, the Chinese outnumber the Malays eight-to-one in science and fifteen-to-one in engineering.[43] In the United States, more than half of all Chinese faculty members teach engineering and the natural sciences,[44] and outside the academic profession, Chinese are similarly concentrated in the same fields.[45] Yet this has been blamed on American society's *excluding* them from other fields.[46] It is a tribute to the power of the civil rights vision that this could be said in all seriousness, even though (1) other fields are generally less well paid than science and engineering, and (2) Chinese Americans as a group earn higher incomes than white Americans.

Germans have historically been notable in the fields of family farming and of industrial technology—both in Germany and in other countries to which they immigrated. German peasants became in the United States the most successful and most numerous of American farmers.[47] They were generally self-employed family farmers, rather than either agricultural laborers or plantation owners. They achieved similarly striking success in family farming in Brazil, Australia, Ireland, and Mexico.[48] Craftsmanship, technology, and science have also been the hallmarks of Germans in Germany—and in the United States, Brazil, Australia, Czechoslovakia, and Chile, among other places.[49] Germans established the piano industry in the United States—and in Australia and in England.[50] In Brazil, the German minority came to own nearly half the industrial enterprises in the southern states, compared to only one-fifth owned by Brazilians of Portuguese ancestry, the majority of the population.[51]

The civil rights vision tends to view group characteristics as mere "stereotypes" and concentrates on changing the public's "perceptions" or raising the public's "consciousness." Yet the reality of group patterns that transcend any given society cannot be denied. Jewish peddlers followed in the wake of the Roman legions and sold goods in the conquered territories.[52] How surprising is it to find Jewish peddlers on the American frontier or on the sidewalks of New York 2,000 years later—or in many other places in between? No one needs to believe that Jews are *genetically* peddlers. But it does suggest that cultural patterns do not readily disappear, either with the passage of time or with social engineering. The very fact that there are still Jews in the world, after centuries of determined efforts to absorb them by church and state alike, implies that environmental influences extend well beyond immediate circumstances— and might better be described as cultural inheritance.

## Politics

Given the civil rights premise that statistical disparities are moral inequities and are caused by social institutions, with group characteristics being derivative from the surrounding society, it follows that the solutions are basically political—changing laws and public perceptions. Political activity thus becomes crucial, with political here being broadly defined to include courts and administrative agencies as well as legislatures, and private institutional activity as well as government policy. As with so many conclusions in this area, the fact that it follows logically from the civil rights vision has largely precluded any apparent need for empirical verification.

Once more looking at this as a general principle, rather than as a projection of the special case of blacks, the question is whether political activity has generally been an important factor in the rise of groups from poverty to prosperity, or in their increased social acceptance. Again, it is an empirical question rather than a foregone conclusion.

Among the groups that have gone into other countries, begun at the bottom and later rose past the original or majority inhabitants are the Chinese in southeast Asia, the Caribbean, and the United States.[53] In all these very different settings, the Chinese have studiously avoided politics. In some countries, such as Malaysia, they have been kept out of politics, but even where political careers were possible the Chinese community leaders have opted to stay out of office-seeking or political agitation. In country after country, they have maintained their own community institutions to adjudicate disputes, care for their needy, and otherwise minimize recourse to the institutions of the surrounding society.[54] *After* achieving affluence and acceptance, some individual Chinese have gone into politics, but typically as representatives of the general population, rather than as ethnic spokesmen. But political activity has played little, if any, role in the often dramatic rises of the Chinese from poverty to affluence.

This pattern has likewise been characteristic of the Germans in the United States, Brazil and Australia. In colonial America, many Germans began as indentured servants, working for years to pay off the cost of their passage across the Atlantic. Most then worked as dirt farmers on frontier land. They were notorious for their *non-*participation in politics in colonial Pennsylvania, where they constituted one-third of the population.[55] Only *after* Germans had risen to prosperity did prominent German political leaders arise. The Muhlenbergs, Carl Schurz, and John Peter Altgeld were the best known in the eighteenth and nineteenth centuries, and Herbert Hoover and Dwight D. Eisenhower in the twentieth century. But as in the case of the Chinese, most of these leaders were by no means primarily spokesmen for German ethnic interests. More important, Germans had risen economically first. The same non-political path to economic advancement was followed by Germans in Brazil and in Australia.[56]

In Argentina, the English immigrants have historically been very successful economically and played a major role in the development of the Argentine economy—but almost no role in Argentine politics.[57]

Jews were for centuries kept out of political rule in a number of countries, either by law, by custom, or by anti-Semitic feelings in the elite or the populace. But even where political careers were at least theoretically open to them, as in the United States, Jews only belatedly sought public office, and in the United States were at first wholly subservient to Irish political bosses. While some Jewish political leaders championed special Jewish causes, the most prominent (Herbert Lehman, and Jacob Javits, for example) were basically spokesmen for more general political causes—and again, by the time that Jews developed political power, they were already well on their way economically. In South Africa, Jews are more prosperous than the ruling Afrikaners, whose policies they have generally opposed, with the result that Jews hold no important political power—certainly none such as could explain their economic advantages. Even in such a free nation as Great Britain, it was the middle of the nineteenth century before the first practicing Jew sat in Parliament, though such converted Jews as Ricardo and Disraeli had been in Parliament earlier in the same century. Yet prosperous Jews were commonplace in Britain long before then.

Until relatively recently, Italians were notorious for non-participation in American politics, and for readily supporting non-Italian candidates over Italian candidates. Even the most famous Italian American politician, Fiorello H. La Guardia, lost the Italian vote to his Irish opponent in 1940,[58] as have other Italian candidates in Chicago, Boston, and elsewhere.[59] In Argentina as well, Italians took

31

little part in political life during their rise from poverty to affluence, though they achieved economic dominance in a number of industries and skilled occupations.[60]

Empirically, political activity and political success have been neither necessary nor sufficient for economic advancement. Nor has eager political participation or outstanding success in politics been translated into faster group achievement. The Irish have been perhaps the most striking example of political success in an ethnic minority, but their rise from poverty was much *slower* than that of other groups who were nowhere near being their political equals. Irish-run political machines dominated many big city governments in America, beginning in the latter part of the nineteenth century, but the great bulk of the Irish populace remained unskilled laborers and domestic servants into the late nineteenth century. The Irish were fiercely loyal to each other, electing, appointing, and promoting their own kind, not only in the political arena but also in the hierarchy of the Catholic Church. This had little effect on the average Irish American, who began to reach economic prosperity in the twentieth century at about the time when the Irish political machines began to decline and when the Irish control of the Catholic Church was increasingly challenged by other ethnic groups.

It would perhaps be easier to find an *inverse* correlation between political activity and economic success than a direct correlation. Groups that have the skills for other things seldom concentrate in politics. Moreover, politics has special disadvantages for ethnic minority groups, however much it may benefit individual ethnic leaders. Public displays of ethnic solidarity and/or chauvinism are the life blood of ethnic politics. Yet chauvinism almost invariably provokes counter-chauvinism.

By the late nineteenth century, the Chinese minority in southeast Asia lived more or less at peace with the majority populations of the various countries of that region. But in the early twentieth century, a new nationalism in China reached out to the overseas Chinese, among other things offering them Chinese citizenship wherever they might live, and interceding on their behalf with the governments of their respective countries of residence. Many of these Chinese had thought of themselves for generations as Siamese, Burmese, etc., but now the resurgent nationalism of China under Sun Yat-sen became their creed as well. Within a few years, the nationalism of China provoked a counter-nationalism among its neighbors in the region, setting in motion increased discrimination and renewed persecution of their Chinese minorities. Successive Chinese governments under Chiang Kai-shek, then Mao-Tse-tung and his successors, have continued this process, provoking continued hostility to the Chinese minorities, culminating in the tragic fate of the "boat people"—most of whom were Chinese—who could find little refuge anywhere because of the general animosity toward them in southeast Asia.

The dialectic of chauvinism and counter-chauvinism was also played out in a very different setting in nineteenth-century Prague, then capital of Bohemia. Here a mixed population—mostly Czech and German—initially thought of themselves simply as Bohemians. But the rise of Czech nationalism and decades of political agitation for specifically Czech causes eventually roused the Germans to abandon their cosmopolitan view of themselves as Bohemians and to organize for specifically German causes.[61] The Czechs won out in the political struggles, especially after the creation of Czechoslovakia following World War I. But the nationalism they had aroused in the Germans came back to haunt them. The politicization and protests of the Sudeten Germans provided the pretext for Hitler's annexation of the Sudeten region of Czechoslovakia as a result of the Munich agreement, which set the stage for World War II.

Polarization by ethnic politics has proven to be easy to achieve in other settings as well, but no comparably easy way has been found to de-polarize peoples. Guyana went from an ethnic coalition government elected in 1953 to a virtually all-black government in 1969, ruling a nation that was half East Indian and only 43 percent black. The rise of counter-extremism among East Indians produced violent clashes in the streets requiring troops to restore order.[62] Blacks and East Indians in Trinidad likewise went from coalition to confrontation in a few years.[63] In the early centuries of Islam, religious minorities were much more tolerated than in later centuries, after the religious zeal of Christians had led to the persecution and expulsion of Muslim communities in Christian lands.[64] In mid-nineteenth-century Britain, the militant, paramilitary Ribbon societies of the Irish Catholic migrants flourished only in those British cities where the militant, paramilitary Orange lodges of the Irish Protestants flourished. Neither became prominent in London, for example, despite a large Irish population there.[65] Chauvinism has bred counter-chauvinism in many historical contexts.

The politicization of race has proven to be explosive, in countries around the world and down through history. Sometimes it is a case of chauvinism provoking counter-chauvinism. At other times, one side may go from quiescence to violence in a very short time, as history is measured. Jews in Germany were so well accepted during the 1920s that they not only achieved many high-level positions but more than half their marriages were with non-Jewish Germans.[66] Yet, just one decade later, resurgent anti-Semitism under the Nazis drove masses of Jews from the country and marked millions of others for the horrors of the Holocaust.

Nor were these merely peculiar depravities of Germans. Historically, Jews had been treated better in Germany than in most of Europe, and German Jews in other countries settled among the German minorities of those countries, where they were welcomed into the cultural and social life of German enclaves.[67] Germans in the United States were also noted historically for their ability to get along with the Indians,[68] and for their opposition to slavery[69] and even support of rights for blacks.[70] If the politicization of race could lead to barbarism and genocide among Germans, no other peoples or society can be presumed to be immune.

However catastrophic the politicization of race may be in the long run, from the point of view of individual leaders it is a highly successful way to rise from obscurity to prominence and power. Those who promoted Czech nationalism in the nineteenth century were typically people from modest social backgrounds,[71] who achieved personal success at the long-run cost of their country's dismemberment and subjugation. Those who have stridently—and sometimes violently—promoted local group preferences in India have likewise typically been from newly educated classes on the rise.[72] Fomenting intergroup hostility has likewise raised many other obscure figures to power in many other countries, from "redneck" politicians in the American South to Idi Amin in Uganda and—the classic example—Adolf Hitler.

In short, despite the unpromising record of politics as a means of raising a group from poverty to affluence, and despite the dangers of politicizing race, there are built-in incentives for individual political leaders to do just that.

## CHAPTER TWO

# FROM EQUAL OPPORTUNITY TO "AFFIRMATIVE ACTION"

The very meaning of the phrase "civil rights" has changed greatly since the *Brown* decision in 1954, or since the Civil Rights Act of 1964. Initially, civil rights meant, quite simply, that all individuals should be treated the same under the law, regardless of their race, religion, sex or other such social categories. For blacks, especially, this would have represented a dramatic improvement in those states where law and public policy mandated racially separate institutions and highly discriminatory treatment.

Many Americans who supported the initial thrust of civil rights, as represented by the *Brown* v. *Board of Education* decision and the Civil Rights Act of 1964, later felt betrayed as the original concept of equal individual *opportunity* evolved toward the concept of equal group *results*. The idea that statistical differences in results were weighty presumptive evidence of discriminatory processes was not initially an explicit part of civil rights law. But neither was it merely an inexplicable perversion, as many critics seem to think, for it followed logically from the civil rights *vision*.

If the causes of intergroup differences can be dichotomized into discrimination and innate ability, then non-racists and non-sexists must expect equal results from non-discrimination. Conversely, the persistence of highly disparate results must indicate that discrimination continues to be pervasive among recalcitrant employers, culturally biased tests, hypocritical educational institutions, etc. The early leaders and supporters of the civil rights movement did not advocate such corollaries, and many explicitly repudiated them, especially during the congressional debates that preceded passage of the Civil Rights Act of 1964.[1] But the corollaries were implicit in the vision—and in the long run that proved to be more decisive than the positions taken by the original leaders in the cause of civil rights. In the face of crying injustices, many Americans accepted a vision that promised to further a noble cause, without quibbling over its assumptions or verbal formulations. But visions have a momentum of their own, and those who accept their assumptions have entailed their corollaries, however surprised they may be when these corollaries emerge historically.

# FROM RIGHTS TO QUOTAS

"Equal opportunity" laws and policies require that individuals be judged on their qualifications as individuals, *without regard* to race, sex, age, etc. "Affirmative action" requires that they be judged *with regard* to such group membership, receiving preferential or compensatory treatment in some cases to achieve a more proportional "representation" in various institutions and occupations.

The conflict between equal opportunity and affirmative action developed almost imperceptibly at first, though it later became a heated issue, repeatedly debated by the time the Civil Rights Act of 1964 was being considered by Congress. The term "affirmative action" was first used in a racial discrimination context in President John F. Kennedy's Executive Order No. 10,925 in 1961. But, as initially presented, affirmative action referred to various activities, such as monitoring subordinate decision makers to ensure the fairness of their hiring and promotion decisions, and spreading information about employment or other opportunities so as to encourage previously excluded groups to apply—after which the actual selection could be made *without regard* to group membership. Thus, it was both meaningful and consistent for President Kennedy's Executive Order to say that federal contractors should "take affirmative action to ensure that the applicants are employed, and that employees are treated during employment, without regard to their race, creed, color, or national origin."

Tendencies toward shifting the emphasis from equality of prospective opportunity toward statistical parity of retrospective results were already observed, at both state and federal levels, by the time that the Civil Rights Act of 1964 was under consideration in Congress. Senator Hubert Humphrey, while guiding this bill through the Senate, assured his colleagues that it "does not require an employer to achieve any kind of racial balance in his work force by giving preferential treatment to any individual or group."[2] He pointed out that subsection 703(j) under Title VII of the Civil Rights Act "is added to state this point expressly."[3] That subsection declared that nothing in Title VII required an employer "to grant preferential treatment to any individual or group on account of any imbalance which may exist" with respect to the numbers of employees in such groups "in comparison with the total number or percentage of persons of such race, color, religion, sex, or national origin in any community, State, section or other area."

39

Virtually all the issues involved in the later controversies over affirmative action, in the specifically numerical sense, were raised in the legislative debates preceding passage of the Civil Rights Act. Under subsection 706(g) of that Act, an employer was held liable only for his own "intentional" discrimination,[4] not for societal patterns reflected in his work force. According to Senator Humphrey, the "express requirement of intent is designed to make it wholly clear that inadvertent or accidental discriminations will not violate the Title or result in the entry of court orders."[5] Vague claims of differential institutional policy impact—"institutional racism"—were not to be countenanced. For example, tests with differential impact on different groups were considered by Humphrey to be "legal unless used for the purpose of discrimination."[6] There was no burden of proof placed upon employers to "validate" such tests.

In general there was to be no burden of proof on employers; rather the Equal Employment Opportunity Commission (EEOC) created by the Act "must prove by a preponderance" that an adverse decision was based on race (or, presumably, other forbidden categories), according to Senator Joseph Clark, another leading advocate of the Civil Rights Act.[7] Senator Clark also declared that the Civil Rights Act "will not require an employer to change existing seniority lists," even though such lists might have differential impact on blacks as the last hired and first fired.[8] Still another supporter, Senator Harrison Williams, declared that an employer with an all-white work force could continue to hire "only the best qualified persons even if they were all white."[9]

In short, Congress declared itself in favor of equal opportunity and opposed to affirmative action. So has the American public. Opinion polls show a majority of blacks opposed to preferential treatment, as is an even larger majority of women.[10] Federal administrative agencies and the

40

courts led the change from the prospective concept of individual equal opportunity to the retrospective concept of parity of group "representation" (or "correction" of "imbalances").

The key development in this process was the creation of the Office of Federal Contract Compliance in the U.S. Department of Labor by President Lyndon Johnson's Executive Order No. 11,246 in 1965. In May 1968, this office issued guidelines containing the fateful expression "goals and timetables" and "representation." But as yet these were still not quotas, for 1968 guidelines spoke of "goals and timetables for the prompt achievement of full and equal employment opportunity." By 1970, however, new guidelines referred to "results-oriented procedures," which hinted more strongly at what was to come. In December 1971, the decisive guidelines were issued, which made it clear that "goals and timetables" were meant to "increase materially the utilization of minorities and women," with "under-utilization" being spelled out as "having fewer minorities or women in a particular job classification than would reasonably be expected by their availability . . ."[11] Employers were required to confess to "deficiencies in the utilization" of minorities and women whenever this statistical parity could not be found in all job classifications, as a first step toward correcting this situation. The burden of proof—and remedy—was on the employer. "Affirmative action" was now decisively transformed into a numerical concept, whether called "goals" or "quotas."[12]

Though lacking in either legislative authorization or public support for numerical group preferences, administrative agencies of government were able to enforce such policies with the support of the federal courts in general and the U.S. Supreme Court in particular. In the landmark *Weber* case the Supreme Court simply rejected "a literal interpretation" of the words of the Civil Rights Act. Instead, it sought the "spirit" of the Act, its "primary concern" with the economic problems of blacks. According to Justice William Brennan, writing the majority opinion, these words do not bar "temporary, voluntary, affirmative action measures undertaken to eliminate manifest racial imbalance in traditionally segregated job categories."[13] This performance received the sarcastic tribute of Justice Rehnquist that it was *"a tour de force* reminiscent not of jurists such as Hale, Holmes, and Hughes but of escape artists such as Houdini."[14] Rehnquist's dissent inundated the Supreme Court with the legislative history of the Act, and Congress' repeated and emphatic rejection of the whole approach of correcting imbalances or compensating for the past.[15] The spirit of the Act was as contrary to the decision as was the letter.

# EQUALITY OF RIGHTS AND RESULTS

Those who carry the civil rights vision to its ultimate conclusion see no great difference between promoting equality of opportunity and equality of results. If there are not equal results among groups presumed to have equal genetic potential, then some inequality of opportunity must have intervened somewhere, and the question of precisely where is less important than the remedy of restoring the less fortunate to their just position. The fatal flaw in this kind of thinking is that there are many reasons, besides genes and discrimination, why groups differ in their economic performances and rewards. Groups differ by large amounts demographically, culturally, and geographically—and all of these differences have profound effects on incomes and occupations.

Age differences are quite large. Blacks are a decade

42

younger than the Japanese. Jews are a quarter of a century older than Puerto Ricans. Polish Americans are twice as old as American Indians.[16] These represent major differences in the quantity of work experience, in an economy where income differences between age brackets are even greater than black-white income differences.[17] Even if the various racial and ethnic groups were identical in every other respect, their age differences alone would prevent their being equally represented in occupations requiring experience or higher education. Their very different age distributions likewise prevent their being equally represented in colleges, jails, homes for the elderly, the armed forces, sports and numerous other institutions and activities that tend to have more people from one age bracket than from another.

Cultural differences add to the age differences. As noted in Chapter 1, half of all Mexican American wives were married in their teens, while only 10 percent of Japanese American wives married that young.[18] Such very different patterns imply not only different values but also very different future opportunities. Those who marry and begin having children earlier face more restricted options for future education and less geographic mobility for seeking their best career opportunities. Even among those young people who go on to colleges and universities, their opportunities to prepare themselves for the better paid professions are severely limited by their previous educational choices and performances, as well as by their selections of fields of study in the colleges and universities. All of these things vary enormously from one group to another.

For example, mathematics preparation and performance differ greatly from one ethnic group to another and between men and women. A study of high school students in northern California showed that four-fifths of Asian youngsters were enrolled in the sequence of mathematics courses that culminate in calculus, while only one-fifth of black

43

youngsters were enrolled in such courses. Moreover, even among those who began this sequence in geometry, the percentage that persisted all the way through to calculus was several times higher among the Asian students.[19] Sex differences in mathematics preparation are comparably large. Among both black and white freshmen at the University of Maryland, the men had had four years of mathematics in high school more than twice as often as the women.[20]

Mathematics is of decisive importance for many more professions than that of mathematician. Whole ranges of fields of study and work are off-limits to those without the necessary mathematical foundation. Physicists, chemists, statisticians, and engineers are only some of the more obvious occupations. In some colleges, one cannot even be an undergraduate economics major without having had calculus, and to go on to graduate school and become a professional economist requires much more mathematics, as well as statistical analysis. Even in fields where mathematics is not an absolute prerequisite, its presence or absence makes a major difference in one's ability to rise in the profession. Mathematics is becoming an important factor in the social sciences and is even beginning to invade some of the humanities. To be mathematically illiterate is to carry an increasing burden into an increasing number of occupations. Even the ability to pass a civil service examination for modest clerical jobs is helped or hindered by one's facility in mathematics.

It is hardly surprising that test scores reflect these group differences in mathematics preparation. Nationwide results on the Scholastic Aptitude Test (SAT) for college applicants show Asians and whites consistently scoring higher on the quantitative test than Hispanics or blacks, and men scoring higher than women.[21] Nor are these differences merely the result of socioeconomic "disadvantage" caused by "society." Black, Mexican American, and American Indian youngsters from families with incomes of $50,000 and up score lower than Asians from families whose incomes are just $6,000 and under.[22] Moreover, Asians as a group score higher than whites as a group on the quantitative portion of the SAT and the Japanese in Japan specialize in mathematics, science and engineering to a far greater extent than do American students in the United States.[23] Cultural differences are real, and cannot be talked away by using pejorative terms such as "stereotypes" or "racism."

The racial, ethnic, and sex differences in mathematics that begin in high school (or earlier) continue on through to the Ph.D. level, affecting career choices and economic rewards. Hispanic Ph.D.'s outnumber Asian Ph.D.'s in the United States by three-to-one in history, but the Asians outnumber the Hispanics by ten-to-one in chemistry.[24] More than half of all Asian Ph.D.'s are in mathematics, science or engineering, and more than half the Asians who teach college teach in those fields. By contrast, more than half of all black doctorates are in the field of education, a notoriously undemanding and less remunerative field. So are half the doctorates received by American Indians, not one of whom received a Ph.D. in either mathematics or physics in 1980.[25] Female Ph.D.'s are in quantitatively-based fields only half as frequently as male Ph.D.'s.[26]

Important as mathematics is in itself, it is also a symptom of broader and deeper disparities in educational choices and performances in general. Those groups with smaller quantities of education tend also to have lower qualities of education, and these disparities follow them all the way through their educational careers and into the job market. The children of lower income racial and ethnic groups typically score lower on tests all through school and attend lower quality colleges when they go to college at all, as well as majoring in the easier courses in fields with the least economic promise. How much of this is due to the home environment and how much to the deficiencies of the public schools in their neighborhoods is a large question that cannot be answered here. But what is clear is that what is called the "same" education, measured in years of schooling, is not even remotely the same in reality.

The civil rights vision relies heavily on statistical "disparities" in income and employment between members of different groups to support its sweeping claims of rampant discrimination. The U.S. Civil Rights Commission, for example, considers itself to be "controlling for those factors"[27] when it examines people of the same age with the same number of years of schooling—resolutely ignoring the substance of that schooling.

Age and education do not begin to exhaust the differences between groups. They are simply more readily quantifiable than some other differences. The geographic distributions of groups also vary greatly, with Mexican Americans being concentrated in the southwest, Puerto Ricans in the northeast, half of blacks in the South, and most Asians in California and Hawaii. Differences in income between the states are also larger than black-white income differences, so that these distributional differences affect national income differences. A number of past studies, for example, have shown black and Puerto Rican incomes to be very similar nationally, but blacks generally earn higher incomes than Puerto Ricans in New York and other places where Puerto Ricans are concentrated.[28] Their incomes nationally have shown up in these studies as similar, because there are very few Puerto Ricans living in low-income southern states.

One of the most important causes of differences in income and employment is the way people work—some diligently, carefully, persistently, cooperatively, and without requiring much supervision or warnings about absenteeism, tardiness, or drinking, and others requiring much such concern over such matters. Not only are such things inherently difficult to quantify; any suggestion that such differences even exist is sure to bring forth a storm of condemnation. In short, the civil rights vision has been hermetically sealed off from any such evidence. Both historical and contemporary observations on intergroup differences in work habits, discipline, reliability, sobriety, cleanliness, or cooperative attitude—anywhere in the world—are automatically dismissed as evidence only of the bias or bigotry of the observers. "Stereotypes" is the magic word that makes thinking about such things unnecessary. Yet despite this closed circle of reasoning that surrounds the civil rights vision, there is some evidence that cannot be disposed of in that way.

Self-employed farmers, for example, do not depend for their rewards on the biases of employers or the stereotypes of observers. Yet self-employed farmers of different ethnicity have fared very differently on the same land, even in earlier pre-mechanization times, when the principal input was the farmer's own labor. German farmers, for example, had more prosperous farms than other farmers in colonial America[29]—and were more prosperous than Irish farmers in eighteenth-century Ireland,[30] as well as more prosperous than Brazilian farmers in Brazil,[31] Mexican farmers in Mexico,[32] Russian farmers in Russia,[33] and Chilean farmers in Chile.[34] We may ignore the forbidden testimony from all these countries as to how hard the German farmers worked, how frugally they lived, or how sober they were. Still, the results speak for themselves.

That Jews earn far higher incomes than Hispanics in the United States might be taken as evidence that anti-Hispanic bias is stronger than anti-Semitism—if one followed the logic of the civil rights vision. But this explanation is considerably weakened by the greater prosperity of Jews than Hispanics *in Hispanic countries* throughout Latin America.[35]

47

Again, even if one dismisses out of hand all the observers who see great differences in the way these two groups work, study, or save, major tangible differences in economic performance remain that cannot be explained in terms of the civil rights vision.

One of the commonly used indices of intergroup economic differences is family income. Yet families are of different sizes from group to group, reflecting differences in the incidence of broken homes. Female headed households are several times more common among blacks than among whites, and in both groups these are the lowest income families. Moreover, the proportion of people working differs greatly from group to group. More than three-fifths of all Japanese American families have multiple income earners while only about a third of Puerto Rican families do. Nor is this a purely socioeconomic phenomenon, as distinguished from a cultural phenomenon. Blacks have similar incomes to Puerto Ricans, but the proportion of black families with a woman working is nearly three times that among Puerto Ricans.[36]

None of this disproves the existence of discrimination, nor is that its purpose. What is at issue is whether statistical differences mean discrimination, or whether there are innumerable demographic, cultural, and geographic differences that make this crucial automatic inference highly questionable.

# EFFECTS VERSUS HOPES

Thus far, we have not even considered the actual effects of the incentives and constraints created by affirmative action policies—as distinguished from the rationales, hopes or claims made for these policies. Because these policies are invoked on behalf of the most disadvantaged groups, and

48

the most disadvantaged classes within these groups, it is especially important to scrutinize the factual record of what has happened to the economic position of such people under both equal opportunity and affirmative policies.

Before crediting either political policy with economic gains, it is worth considering what trends were already under way before they were instituted. Much has been made of the number of blacks in high-level occupations before and after the Civil Rights Act of 1964. What has been almost totally ignored is the historical *trend* of black representation in such occupations before the Act was passed. In the period from 1954 to 1964, for example, the number of blacks in professional, technical, and similar high-level positions more than doubled.[37] In other kinds of occupations, the advance of blacks was even greater during the 1940s—when there was little or no civil rights policy— than during the 1950s when the civil rights revolution was in its heyday.[38]

The rise in the number of blacks in professional and technical occupations in the two years from 1964 to 1966 (after the Civil Rights Act) was in fact *less* than in the one year from 1961 to 1962 (before the Civil Rights Act).[39] If one takes into account the growing black population by looking at percentages instead of absolute numbers, it becomes even clearer that the Civil Rights Act of 1964 represented no acceleration in trends that had been going on for many years. The percentage of employed blacks who were professional and technical workers rose less in the five years following the Civil Rights Act of 1964 than in the five years preceding it. The percentage of employed blacks who were managers and administrators was the same in 1967 as in 1964—and in 1960. Nor did the institution of "goals and timetables" at the end of 1971 mark any acceleration in the long trend of rising black representation in these occupations. True, there was an appreciable increase in the per-

49

centage of blacks in professional and technical fields from 1971 to 1972, but almost entirely offset by a reduction in the percentage of blacks who were managers and administrators.[40]

The history of Asians and Hispanics likewise shows long-term upward trends that began years before the Civil Rights Act of 1964 and were not noticeably accelerated by the Act or by later "affirmative action" policies. The income of Mexican Americans rose relative to that of non-Hispanic whites between 1959 and 1969 (after the Civil Rights Act), but no more so than from 1949 to 1959 (before the Act).[41] Chinese and Japanese Americans overtook other Americans in income by 1959—five years before the Civil Rights Act.

Ignoring trends already in progress for years makes before-and-after comparisons completely misleading. Yet that is precisely the approach of supporters of the civil rights vision, who proceed as if "before" was a static situation. Yet the notion that the Civil Rights Act and "affirmative action" have had a dramatic impact on the economic progress of minorities has become part of the folklore of the land, established primarily through repetition and vehemence, rather than evidence.

The evidence of the *political* impact of civil rights changes in the 1960s is far more clear-cut. The number of black elected officials, especially in the South, increased manyfold in a relatively few years, including blacks elected to public office in some places for the first time since the Reconstruction era after the Civil War. Perhaps even more important, white elected officials in the South had to change both their policies and their rhetoric to accommodate the new political reality that blacks could vote.

What is truly surprising—and relatively ignored—is the economic impact of affirmative action on the disadvantaged, for whom it is most insistently invoked. The relative

50

position of disadvantaged individuals within the groups singled out for preferential treatment has generally *declined* under affirmative action. This is particularly clear in data for individuals, as distinguished from families.

Family income data have too many pitfalls to be taken at face value. There are, for example, significant variations in what constitutes a family, both from time to time and from group to group. But since many people insist on using such data, these statistics cannot be passed over in silence. In 1969, *before* the federal imposition of numerical "goals and timetables," Puerto Rican family income was 63 percent of the national average. By 1977, it was down to 50 percent. In 1969, Mexican American family income was 76 percent of the national average. By 1977 it was down to 73 percent. Black family income fell from 62 percent of the national average to 60 percent over the same span.[42]

There are many complex factors behind these numbers. The point here is simply that they do not support the civil rights vision. A finer breakdown of the data for blacks shows the most disadvantaged families—the female-headed, with no husband present—to be not only the poorest and with the slowest increase in money income during the 1970s (a decline in *real* income) but also with money incomes increasing even more slowly than among white, female-headed families. By contrast, black husband-wife families had money incomes that were rising faster than that of their white counterparts.[43] It is part of a more general pattern of the most disadvantaged falling farther behind during the affirmative action era, while the already advantaged forged ahead.

Individual data tell the same story, even more clearly. Those blacks with less education and less job experience—the truly disadvantaged—have been falling farther and farther behind their white counterparts under affirmative action, during the very same years when blacks with more

51

education and more job experience have been advancing economically, both absolutely and relative to their white counterparts. First, the disadvantaged: Black male high school dropouts with less than six years of work experience earned 79 percent of the income of white male high school dropouts with less than six years of work experience in 1967 (before affirmative action quotas) and this *fell* to 69 percent by 1978 (after affirmative action quotas). Over these very same years, the income of black males who had completed college and had more than six years of work experience *rose* from 75 percent of the income of their white counterparts to 98 percent.[44] Some economic trends can be explained in terms of general conditions in the economy, but such diametrically opposite trends during the very same span of years obviously cannot.

There is additional evidence that the advantaged have benefited under affirmative action while the disadvantaged have fallen behind. Black faculty members with numerous publications and Ph.D.'s from top-rated institutions earned more than white faculty members with the same high qualifications, but black faculty members who lacked a doctorate or publications earned less than whites with the same low qualifications.[45] The pattern of diametrically opposite trends in economic well-being among advantaged and disadvantaged blacks is also shown by the general internal distribution of income among blacks. The top fifth of blacks have absorbed a growing proportion of all income received by blacks, while each of the bottom three fifths has received declining shares.[46] Black college-educated couples with husband and wife working had by 1980 achieved incomes higher than white couples of the same description.[47] Meanwhile, at the other end of the spectrum, the black female-headed household was receiving only 62 percent of the income of white, female-headed households—down from 70 percent in 1970.[48]

None of this is easily reconcilable with the civil rights vision's all-purpose explanation, racism and discrimination. To explain such diametrically opposite trends within the black community on the basis of whites' behavior would require us to believe that racism and discrimination were growing and declining at the same time. It is much more reconcilable with ordinary economic analysis.

Affirmative action hiring pressures make it costly to have no minority employees, but continuing affirmative action pressures at the promotion and discharge phases also make it costly to have minority employees who do not work out well. The net effect is to increase the demand for highly qualified minority employees while decreasing the demand for less qualified minority employees or for those without a sufficient track record to reassure employers.

Those who are most vocal about the need for affirmative action are of course the more articulate minority members —the advantaged who speak in the name of the disadvantaged. Their position on the issue may accord with their own personal experience, as well as their own self-interest. But that cannot dismiss the growing evidence that it is precisely the disadvantaged who suffer from affirmative action.

# BY THE NUMBERS

## Averages versus Variance

One of the remarkable aspects of affirmative action is that, while numbers—and *assumptions* about numbers—abound, proponents of the program are almost never challenged to produce positive numerical evidence for its effectiveness or to support their statistical presuppositions. The mere fact that some group is $x$ percent of the population but only $y$ percent of the employees is taken as weighty presumption of employer discrimination. There are serious statistical problems with this approach, quite aside from substantial group differences in age, education, and cultural values.

Even in a random world of identical things, to say that something happens a certain way *on the average* is not to say that it happens that way *every time.* But affirmative action deals with averages almost as if there were no variance. If Hispanics are 8 percent of the carpenters in a given town, it does not follow that *every* employer of carpenters in that town would have 8 percent Hispanics if there were no discrimination. Even if carpenters were assigned to employers by drawing lots (or by some other random process), there would be *variance* in the proportion of Hispanic carpenters from one employer to another. To convict those employers with fewer Hispanics of discrimination in hiring would be to make statistical variance a federal offense.

To illustrate the point, we can consider some process where racial, sexual, or ideological factors do not enter, such as the flipping of a coin. There is no reason to expect a persistent preponderance of heads over tails (or vice versa) on the *average,* but there is also no reason to expect exactly half heads and half tails every time we flip a coin a few times. That is, *variance* will exist.

To illustrate the effect of statistical variance, a coin was flipped ten times and then this experiment was repeated ten times. Here are the results:

| HEADS | 3 | 4 | 3 | 4 | 6 | 7 | 2 | 4 | 5 | 3 |
|-------|---|---|---|---|---|---|---|---|---|---|
| TAILS | 7 | 6 | 7 | 6 | 4 | 3 | 8 | 6 | 5 | 7 |

At one extreme, there were seven heads and three tails, and at the other extreme eight tails and two heads. Statistics not only have averages, they have variance.

Translate this into employment decisions. Imagine that

you are the employer who ends up with eight employees from one group and two from another, even though both groups are the same size and no different in qualifications, and even though you have been unbiased in selecting. Try explaining to EEOC and the courts that you ended up with four times as many employees from one group by random chance! You may be convicted of discrimination, even if you have only been guilty of statistical variance.

Of course some employers are biased, just as some coins are biased because of the way their weight is distributed on the design. This particular coin might have been biased; over all, it came up heads 41 percent of the time and tails 59 percent. But even if the coin was biased toward tails, it still came up heads seven times out of ten in one set of flips. If an employer were similarly biased in *favor* of a particular group, he could still be convicted of discrimination *against* that very group, if they ended up with less than half the "representation" of some other group.

No one needs to assume that this particular coin was unbiased or even that the results were accurately reported. Anyone can collect ten people and have them flip a coin ten times, to see the statistical variance for himself. Frivolous as this might seem, the results have deadly serious implications for the way people are convicted of violating federal laws, regulations, and guidelines. It might be especially instructive if this little experiment were performed by editorial writers for publications that fervently support affirmative action, or by clerks of the Supreme Court.

Even when conclusions are based only on differences that statisticians call "statistically significant," this by no means eliminates the basic problem. What is statistically significant depends upon the probability that such a result would have happened by random chance. A common litmus test used by statisticians is whether the event would occur more than 5 times out of a hundred by random chance. Applying this common test of statistical significance to affirmative action means that even in the most extreme case imaginable—zero discrimination and zero difference among racial, ethnic, and other groups—the EEOC could still run 10,000 employers' records through a computer and come up with about 500 "discriminators."

The illustration chosen is in fact too favorable to the proponents of affirmative action, because it shows the probability of incorrectly calling an employer a discriminator when there is only *one* group in question that might be discriminated against. Affirmative action has a number of groups whose statistical employment patterns can lead to charges of discrimination. To escape a false charge of discrimination, an employer must avoid being in the fatal 5 percent for *all* the groups in question simultaneously. That becomes progressively harder when there are more groups.

While there is a 95 percent chance for a non-discriminatory employer to escape when there is only one group, this falls to 86 percent when there are three separate groups and to 73 percent when there are six.[49] That is, even in a world of zero discrimination and zero differences among groups, more than one-fourth of all employers would be called "discriminators" by this common test of statistical significance, when there are six separate groups in question.

What this means is that the courts have sanctioned a procedure which insures that large-scale statistical "discrimination" will exist forever, regardless of what the actual facts may be. They have made statistical variance a federal offense.[50]

## Shopping for Discrimination

Often the very same raw data point to different conclusions at different levels of aggregation. For example, statistics have shown that black faculty members earn less than white faculty members, but as these data are broken down by field of specialization, by number of publications, by possession (or non-possession) of a Ph.D. and by the ranking of the institution that issued it, then the black-white income difference not only shrinks but disappears, and in some fields reverses—with black faculty earning more than white faculty with the same characteristics.[51] For those who accept statistics as proof of discrimination, how much discrimination there is, and in what direction, depends upon how finely these data are broken down.

There is no "objective" or "scientific" way to decide at what level of aggregation to stop breaking the data down into finer categories. Nor have the laws or the courts specified in advance what will and will not be the accepted way to break down the statistics. Any individual or organization contemplating a lawsuit against an employer can arrange that employer's statistics in any number of possible ways and then go shopping among the possibilities for the one that will present the employment pattern in the worst light. This is a very effective strategy in a society in which groups differ enormously in their characteristics and choices, while the prevailing vision makes deviations from a random distribution evidence against the employer.

A discrimination case can depend entirely on what level of statistical breakdown the judge accepts, for different groups will be represented—or "under-represented"—differently according to how precisely occupations and qualifications are defined. While there were more black than Asian American "social scientists" receiving a Ph.D. in

1980, when social scientists were broken down further, there were nearly three times as many Asian as black *economists.*[52] While male recipients of Ph.D.'s in the social sciences outnumbered female recipients of Ph.D.'s by slightly less than two-to-one in 1980, men outnumbered women by more than four-to-one among doctorates in economics and by ten-to-one among doctorates in econometrics.[53] What is the employer hiring: social scientists, economists or econometricians? He may in fact be looking for an econometrician specializing in international trade—and there may be no statistics available on that. Nor can anyone infer the proportion of women or minority members available in that specialty from their distribution in broader categories, for the distribution changes at every level of aggregation.

The same principle applies in other fields as well. A computer manufacturer who is looking for an engineer is not looking for the same kind of engineer as a company that builds bridges. Nor is there the slightest reason to expect all groups to be distributed the same in these sub-specialties as they are among engineers in general. Even within a narrow occupational range such as mathematical specialists, blacks outnumber Asian Americans in gross numbers but Asian Americans outnumber blacks more than two-to-one among statisticians.[54]

When comparing any employer's work force with the available labor pool to determine "under-representation," everything depends on how that labor pool is defined—at what level of aggregation. Those who wish to argue for discrimination generally prefer broad, loose, heterogeneous categories. The concept of a "qualified" worker aids that approach. When the barely qualified is treated as being the same as the most highly skilled and experienced, it is the same as staying at a very general level of aggregation. Anything that creates or widens the disparity between what the job requires and how the categories are defined increases the potential for statistical "discrimination."

An employer may be guilty or innocent according to what level of statistical aggregation a judge accepts, after the plaintiffs have shopped around among the many possibilities. But that is only part of the problem. A more fundamental problem is that *the burden of proof is on the accused* to prove his innocence, once suspicious numbers have been found. Shopping around for suspicious numbers is by no means difficult, especially for a federal agency, given statistical variance, multiple groups, multiple occupations, and wide-ranging differences in the characteristics and choices of the groups themselves.

Statistical aggregation is a major factor not only in courts of law but also in the court of public opinion. Many statistics from a very general level of aggregation are repeatedly presented in the media as demonstrating pervasive discrimination. The finer breakdowns are more likely to appear in specialized scholarly journals, read by a relative handful of people. Yet these finer breakdowns of statistics often tell a drastically different story, not only for black-white differences and male-female differences but for other groups as well.

For example, American Indian males earn significantly less than white males, and Asian males earn significantly more. Yet, as one holds a wide range of variables constant, these income differences shrink to the vanishing point. Asian Americans, for example, are distributed geographically in a very different pattern from whites. Asians are concentrated in higher income states, in more urban areas, and have more education. When all of this is held constant, their income advantage vanishes.[55] By the same token, when various demographic and cultural variables—notably proficiency in the English language—are held constant, the income disadvantages of Hispanic and American Indian males also disappear.[56]

It can hardly be expected that discrimination lawsuits and discrimination as a political issue will be correspondingly reduced any time soon. The methods by which it is measured in the courts and in politics insures that it will be a continuing source of controversy.

Poverty and huge intergroup differences in income are serious matters, whether or not discrimination is the cause —and whether or not affirmative action is the cure. Yet any attempt to deal with these very real disadvantages must first cut through the fog generated by a vision more powerful than its evidence—and, in fact, a vision shaping what courts will accept as evidence.

## CHAPTER THREE

# FROM SCHOOL DESEGREGATION TO BUSING

One of the oldest legal maxims is that "hard cases make bad law." Courts confronted with someone in an impossible situation may be sorely tempted to make a decision to relieve his distress, even if that requires bending the law in ways that may turn out to be catastrophic in the long run.

*Brown* v. *Board of Education* was a hard case in two very different senses. Segregation and discrimination against blacks, in the South especially, was a national scandal and an international embarrassment to the United States. Increasing numbers of people, even among white southerners, were beginning to question it. In Washington, D.C.— still very much a white southern city in mid-century America—segregated public accommodations were voluntarily desegregated two years before the historic 1954 decision. The public humiliation of blacks was clearly not something that could continue to be countenanced indefinitely. *How* to end racial segregation and discrimination, consistent with existing law and judicial precedent, was what made it a hard case.

What also made it a hard case was the virtual certainty of massive resistance among white segregationists who dominated the southern political, judicial, economic, and social scene. For the U.S. Supreme Court to issue a decree that

61

would be evaded, nullified and mocked would be not only a bitter setback for the cause of civil rights but, in addition, a catastrophic undermining of the authority of the courts in general.

Within these severe constraints, the Supreme Court had to shape a decision for the case before them—a little girl named Linda Brown, denied admission to the all-white school near her home and forced to take a bus to an all-black school in another neighborhood. It was, of course, also the case of millions of other blacks, forced to endure a wide range of Jim Crow laws.

More than half a century earlier, another Supreme Court had said that "separate but equal" facilities were Constitutional and met the Fourteenth Amendment's requirement of "equal protection of the laws." Was the 1954 Court to say that the earlier Court was simply wrong, that the whole southern legal system was wrong—and indeed, that the "southern way of life" was wrong? And if so, on what authority—that is, on what authority that would be sufficiently respected to overcome the stubborn resistance of segregationists? It was, in short, a political as well as a legal dilemma. A strong dissenting opinion, even of one Justice, could fuel southern segregationist demagoguery and stiffen resistance for decades. The decision had to be one that all the Justices would accept, that much of the public could accept, and that the Executive Branch would enforce.

This was the hard case that provided both the law and the vision behind the civil rights revolution.

The Supreme Court did not simply repudiate their predecessors as wrong-headed. Chief Justice Earl Warren was also particularly concerned that the approach to the South be "non-accusatory."[1] Instead, he invoked something called "modern authority," which had, by research, demonstrated that separate schools were *inherently* unequal in educational results. Therefore, it was *now* necessary to begin to desegregate the schools in order to meet the Fourteenth Amendment's requirement of "equal protection" under the laws. Their predecessors could not have been expected to know what "modern authority" had so recently revealed, nor was it necessary to condemn the South for not having had this revelation earlier. Apparently nobody was really to blame—but the change had to be made anyway. It was a political masterpiece, under the pressures of the times. Whether it makes sense in terms of logic, evidence, or later consequences is another question.

*Brown* v. *Board of Education* contained not only the general civil rights vision but also added a new educational doctrine of its own—that the separateness of education necessarily rendered it unequal:

> To separate them from others of similar age and qualifications solely because of race generates a feeling of inferiority as to their status in the community that may affect their hearts and minds in a way unlikely ever to be undone.[2]

Warren then quoted with approval a lower court judge's statement: "A sense of inferiority affects the motivation of the child to learn." According to the Chief Justice, "this finding is amply supported by modern authority." Following this logic, he concluded: "Separate educational facilities are inherently unequal." Damage to the self-esteem and/or educational performance of minority children renders "separate but equal" education a contradiction in terms, even if the outward physical facilities or other tangible factors are comparable. This made it unnecessary to be "accusatory," to go into the cynical abuse of the "separate but equal" doctrine in the South or to criticize the previous Supreme Court that created this legal fiction in innocence of "modern authority" for the Court's psychological pronouncement.

"Modern authority" was revealed in a footnote to the

*Brown* decision to be studies suggesting that black children held their own race in low esteem. Similar results have been found in other studies, in both the North and the South, in both segregated and integrated school systems, and among children too young to have attended any school.[3] Indeed, similar findings in both segregated and unsegregated schools had appeared earlier in the writings of the first "modern authority" cited in the Supreme Court decision, Kenneth B. Clark.[4] Innumerable subsequent studies of the self-esteem of black youngsters in integrated school settings have shown no general pattern of higher self-esteem. Some studies show less self-esteem, some show more, and other studies show mixed results.[5] "Modern authority" may have been more politically acceptable than a frontal assault on Jim Crow, but its factual and logical basis was hardly solid.

In the fervor of the times, this might have seemed like nit-picking, but in the longer run the assumptions embedded in this decision have continued to haunt school desegregation, and to embroil public schools in controversy, long after the desegregation of other American institutions has become an accepted fact. An airport, a hospital, or a sports arena is considered desegregated when everyone has an *opportunity* to use it, regardless of what proportions of people from what groups actually use it. But a school with exactly the same racial proportions as an audience attending an opera or passengers using Dulles Airport could easily be served with a federal court order to desegregate, while these other institutions would not be. The conflict between opportunity and results is nowhere more acute than in school desegregation cases.

Here again, it is necessary to emphasize that the Supreme Court's doctrine was not limited to blacks but was a general pronouncement about the psychological and educational effects of one-group schools. Implicitly in logic and historically in practice, this meant that schools had to have racially mixed student bodies—or else they were unequal, and therefore violated the "equal protection of the law" required by the Fourteenth Amendment. Initially, this was not a conclusion stated by the Court or asked for by the NAACP attorneys. Indeed the attorneys denied any such claim in the *Brown* case.[6] But as in the case of affirmative action, the explicit statements, or even honest convictions, of the initial civil rights advocates meant less in the long run than the implicit logic of the civil rights vision as it unfolded over time.

# FROM BROWN TO GREEN—AND BEYOND

The Supreme Court began very cautiously to implement the *Brown* decision. Because of "the great variety of local conditions,"[7] it postponed action after announcing its decision, and scheduled extensive discussions with state and local officials on how to implement its verdict. More than a year passed before they issued a new decree. In the meantime, various segregated school systems began voluntarily desegregating in Washington, Baltimore, Louisville, St. Louis, and in parts of West Virginia, Texas, Arkansas and Delaware.[8] But in other places, particularly in the deep South, opposition was so adamant that, ten years after *Brown,* less than 2 percent of black children in the states of the old Confederacy had white classmates.[9]

In the early years, the Supreme Court proceeded warily to pick its way through the opposition, defiance, and evasions. The implementing decree of May 31, 1955 authorized the lower courts to issue orders and decrees to admit children to public schools "on a racially non-discriminatory basis with all deliberate speed." This gave lower courts room to maneuver, to press for school desegregation where it looked as though judicial pressure would be sufficient, without requiring the courts to run into a brick wall where the local prospects were not promising. Although the Supreme Court later excluded "hostility to racial desegregation"[10] as a factor to be taken into account, that was clearly a major—if not overwhelming—factor in decisions as to when and where "all deliberate speed" meant *now*. Finally, the decentralization of judicial action on racial desegregation defused the accusation that this was all the arbitrary doings of nine men in Washington.

Yet the decentralization was more apparent than real, more form than substance. By deciding which judges' procedures and interpretations to accept and which to overrule, the Supreme Court continued making local as well as national decisions, while verbally seeming to grant broad discretion to the lower courts. For example when federal Judge John Parker ruled in 1955 that *Brown* required non-discrimination and no denial of public access to any public school on the basis of race—*but not a positive attempt to mix races*—his decision was allowed to stand, though it spawned innumerable evasions throughout the South.[11] Yet by 1968, after the political climate had changed, this interpretation was repudiated entirely by the Supreme Court—and again, by making it appear to be a lower court decision.

The key case grew out of the Civil Rights Act of 1964. That Act was as unequivocal on school desegregation as it was on employment policy that equal opportunity did *not* mean prescribed results. The floor manager of the bill in the House of Representatives, Congressman Emanuel Celler, declared that this law contained "no authorization" for federal officials to move toward "achieving racial balance in given schools."[12] This view was echoed by other supporters of the Civil Rights Act, including Senate floor manager Hubert Humphrey, as they sought the votes for its passage.[13] Humphrey assured the Senate that "while the Constitution prohibits segregation, it does not require integration."[14] But again, despite the assurance preceding passage of the Civil Rights Act, subsequent decisions by administrative agencies and the courts went directly counter to such assurances.

When the Fifth Circuit Court of Appeals declared that "we use the words 'integration' and 'desegregation' interchangeably," its ruling was directly the opposite of the interpretation of all the other circuits and of those who wrote the Civil Rights Act. But merely by refusing to review the Fifth Circuit decree, the Supreme Court changed the whole meaning of desegregation, without having to be overtly involved. It then agreed to hear appeals from the other Circuit Court decisions, and quickly overruled their contrary interpretations as they were appealed.[15] It was masterful as political maneuvering, whatever its merits or demerits as law or social policy.

Finally, in 1968, the Supreme Court struck openly and decisively for the racial mixing of schools. A Virginia school district that had formerly been segregated was operating with an open-enrollment or "free choice" system, in which it provided transportation to any child wishing to enroll in any school in the district. Only a fraction of the black children enrolled in the schools that had previously been all white and no white children enrolled in the black school. Whether this school district was "segregated" or not depended entirely on whether segregation was defined in terms of opportunity or results.

Because those who sued for a more sweeping racial integration order had conceded that their choice of schools was "unrestricted and unencumbered," in the words of the Circuit Court of Appeals, it ruled against them in the case of *Green* v. *County School Board of New Kent County*. But the U.S.

Supreme Court overruled the Circuit Court of Appeals. According to the Supreme Court, there was now an "affirmative duty" to eliminate "dual" school systems "root and branch."[16] The specific meaning of "dual school system" was clarified by the Court's example that only 15 percent of black children attended the white school.[17] In other words, statistical *results* defined segregation.

*Green* was in many ways as decisive a case as *Brown*. It opened the era of court-ordered busing to remedy racial imbalance. The Court and its supporters represented this as simply speeding up the process begun long before under the doctrine of "all deliberate speed," which now was regarded as "no longer constitutionally permissible." In reality, however, it was a substitution of a very different process —one in which children were to be assigned to schools by race instead of *without regard* to race. In yet another sense, however, all this was implicit in *Brown* from the outset. If it was the separation that made schools inferior, thereby violating the Fourteenth Amendment, then only "integrated" schools could provide "equality" in education. It may not have been politic to have said this openly from the outset, but that was the inherent logic of the argument. It was no accident that those who accepted the premises were led in that direction, whether they were in administrative agencies or the courts.

As the courts proceeded to order busing of a more and more sweeping nature, under a wider variety of circumstances, the original rationale of dismantling previously segregated school systems (as in *Green*) began to wear very thin. Compulsory busing orders were upheld by the Supreme Court even in states that had never assigned students by race and which even had legal prohibitions against racial assignments long before *Brown* v. *Board.*[18] Clearly, racial mixing was considered "a good thing," to be upheld by such ad hoc reasons as could be found.

Thirty years after *Brown* v. *Board* is surely not too soon to inquire into this assumption, which is crucial from the standpoint of logic, whether or not it was in reality no more than a convenient way to avoid being "accusatory" while striking down racial segregation.

# ASSUMPTIONS VERSUS HISTORY

The central assumption behind busing was perhaps nowhere better expressed than by Los Angeles Judge Paul V. Egly, when he declared that minority students would be "irreparably damaged" if busing were even delayed, and that his task was to "make the most efficient use of increasingly scarce white students as possible"[19] by spreading them around for the benefit of the many minority youngsters who constituted a majority of that city's school children. Kipling's doctrine of "the white man's burden" was now transformed into a judicial doctrine of the white child's burden—a doctrine that came very close to fighting racism with racism.

The actual history of racial and ethnic education in the United States has played remarkably little role in the sweeping theories and pronouncements behind court-ordered busing—except in the special case of blacks, where one-group schools were only part of a much larger and more complex system of oppression under Jim Crow laws. Yet, for purposes of busing orders, "minority" children include Hispanics and Asians—even though the latter often out-perform the white children who are depicted as an urgent necessity for their education. Yet, in another sense, inclusion of the Asians is perfectly consistent. Under the assumptions of the civil rights vision, Asians as non-whites should *not* be doing as well in school as they do, just as they should not be doing as well as they do in the job market.

69

The question, then, is whether assumptions are to be accepted for their plausibility and their conformity to a larger social vision, or whether even the most plausible and satisfying assumptions must nevertheless be forced to confront actual facts.

The most casual knowledge of history shows that all-Jewish, all-Chinese, or all-German schools have not been inherently inferior. The more general question is whether (1) ethnic minority youngsters in general perform better when scattered among the general school population or when concentrated in their own schools, and (2) whether the educational disparities found between segregated blacks and whites are of a different magnitude than educational differences found between other ethnic groups living in the same neighborhoods and going to the same schools.

Data collected for several American ethnic groups, and going back several decades, show that youngsters of Mexican, Chinese, American Indian, and Puerto Rican ancestry scored just as high (or higher) on tests when they went to schools that were virtually all of their own group as they scored in society at large.[20] The same data also showed test score differences between Japanese American and Mexican American youngsters attending the same schools to be as great as those between blacks and whites attending segregated schools in the South.[21] Even larger differences were found between Jews and Puerto Ricans attending the same school over a period of twenty years.[22] Moreover, differences between some all black, legally segregated schools were as great or greater than the average difference between blacks and whites in segregated schools.[23]

In short, group disparities and even intragroup disparities are both large and commonplace, whether or not segregation is involved. In the early twentieth century, Jewish and German youngsters in New York City completed high school at a rate more than one hundred times that among

Irish and Italian youngsters.[24] Chinese and Japanese school children were at one time segregated both *de facto* and *de jure* in California,[25] yet they outperformed white children —and largely still do.[26]

# THE TANGLED WEB

The tortuous evolution of the law from *Brown* to *Green* and its sequels has been a painful reminder of the truth of Sir Walter Scott's immortal lines:

> Oh, what a tangled web we weave,
> When first we practice to deceive!

That the deception may have been for noble purposes and under dire stresses has not prevented *Brown* v. *Board* from leading to the tangled web of school busing. Psychological doctrine, without foundation in logic or law, was used to circumvent the wrath of segregationists. But this doctrine, once conjured up, has taken its own course—and has also taken its toll on the school systems and on the social fabric of the nation.

The case against segregation is that it is both wrong and socially dangerous for the state to classify people by race for different treatment. The pretense that "modern authority" provides a different rationale was an expedient that has continued to haunt school desegregation and keep it embittered and counterproductive. Other institutions have been desegregated years ago with nothing like the social malaise that surrounds busing. But desegregation for other institutions means simply opening the doors to all, regardless of how many from what groups choose to come in. Other institutions do not need to follow the theories of "modern authority."

71

By *logically* basing its decisions on the unsubstantiated conclusions of selected intellectuals—whatever it may have been based on in reality[27]—the Supreme Court set a precedent that continues to dominate busing cases. In such cases, "experts" continue to weave elaborate webs of fragile plausibilities, complete with graphs, equations, jargon—and contradictory conclusions. Ironically, the chief authority cited in *Brown*—the study by Kenneth B. Clark—has been devastated by later criticism from other scholars,[28] and was regarded as a "gimmick" even by NAACP lawyers in the case, one of whom in later years admitted: "I may have used the word 'crap'."[29]

## CHAPTER FOUR

# THE SPECIAL CASE OF BLACKS

Blacks have a history in the United States that is quite different from that of other American ethnic groups. The massive fact of slavery looms over more than half of that history. The Jim Crow laws and policies, which not only segregated but discriminated, were still going strong in that part of the country where most blacks lived, in the middle of the twentieth century. "Lynching" meant—almost invariably—the lynching of blacks by whites. Blacks were widely believed to be genetically inferior in intelligence, both in the North and the South, long before Arthur Jensen's writings on the subject appeared. James B. Conant's 1961 book, *Slums and Suburbs,* reported a common assumption among school officials around the country that black children were not capable of learning as much as white children.[1]

Blacks are also black for life. They do not have the option simply to change their names and life-styles and blend into the general population—or to reserve their ethnicity for special occasions like St. Patrick's Day or Columbus Day.

Thus far we have questioned the validity and appropriateness of shaping a general civil rights vision, as the law of the land for all groups, from the highly unusual experience of blacks. Now the question can be confronted as to how well that vision serves the group in whose name it was first invoked.

Given the unique—and uniquely oppressive—history of blacks, it would follow almost inevitably from the civil rights vision that blacks would today suffer far more than other groups from low income, broken homes, and the whole litany of social pathology. But like so many things that follow from the civil rights vision, it happens not to be true in fact. Blacks do not have the lowest income,[2] the lowest educational level,[3] or the most broken homes[4] among American ethnic groups. The habit of comparing blacks with "the national average" conceals the fact that there are other groups with very similar—and sometimes worse—social pathology. The national average is just one point on a wide-ranging spectrum. It is not a norm showing where most individuals or most groups are. The difference in income between Japanese Americans and Puerto Ricans is even greater than the difference between blacks and whites, though most of the factors *assumed* to cause black-white differences are not present in differences between Japanese Americans and Puerto Ricans.

Internationally, blacks in Latin America have not been subjected to as rigid and severe segregation, oppression, or violence as blacks in the United States. Yet blacks in Brazil, for example, are economically farther behind whites than are blacks in the United States,[5] even though Brazil is widely recognized as having better race relations than the U.S. Both the domestic and the international examples suggest that what is most dramatic, most historic, or most morally revolting need not coincide with what is most economically determining.

In short, the historical uniqueness of blacks has not translated into a contemporary uniqueness in incomes, occupations, I.Q., unemployment, female-headed households, alcoholism, or welfare dependency, however much blacks

74

may differ from the mythical national average in these respects. All of these represent serious difficulties (sometimes calamities) for blacks, and indirectly for the larger society, but the question here is the *cause*. If that cause is either a unique history or a unique genetics, blacks would differ not only from the national average but also from other groups that share neither that history nor the same genetic background.

To take one of the most blatant and most controversial examples, the average I.Q. score of blacks in the United States has been about 85 over the years,[6] compared to a national norm of 100. Groups with average I.Q.'s of 85 have been common in American history and in many other countries as well. These include Catholics in northern Ireland,[7] inhabitants of the Hebrides islands off Scotland,[8] white mountaineers in the United States,[9] and people in canal boat communities in Britain.[10] Back around World War I, such groups included such immigrant groups as the Italians, Poles, and Greeks, most of whom today score at or above 100 on I.Q. tests.[11]

Nowhere has the "legacy of slavery" argument been used more sweepingly than in explaining the high incidence of broken homes, female-headed households, and teenage pregnancy among contemporary blacks. As in so many other areas, the power of a vision is shown not by the evidence marshaled to support it but precisely by the *absence* of any perceived need to supply evidence. The first serious factual study of black family patterns from slavery through the twentieth century was published in 1976. Its masses of data devastated the prevailing beliefs that had been repeated uncritically for generations. Most black children, even under slavery, grew up in two-parent households.[12] A teenage girl raising a child with no man present was a rarity among blacks, both during the era of slavery and as late as the 1920s.[13] Even today, when this

75

phenomenon has become widespread and catastrophic among blacks, it is even more prevalent among Puerto Ricans.[14]

Blacks are indeed a special case. But to say that blacks literally cannot be compared to other groups is to say that we must remain ignorant of how much that special history has to do with contemporary social phenomena. Or else we must accept foregone conclusions based on a vision rather than on facts.

If comparisons were being made for the trivial purpose of some kind of invidious game, then it would of course make no sense, for example, to compare blacks with Jews, who were freed from slavery thousands of years ago. Nor would it make much sense to urge blacks to blind imitation of what someone else did in the nineteenth century under entirely different circumstances. The media seem particularly prone to translate causal analysis as this kind of advice —and to attribute such advice to anyone who has made such analysis.[15] Even writers who have specifically emphasized the changes in the economy since the nineteenth century[16] are depicted as urging twentieth-century blacks to follow nineteenth-century paths—paths that no longer exist.

Blacks can no more become Irish than the Irish can become Chinese. What we can all do, however, is become better informed as to what factors play what role in social phenomena—using the experience of the Irish, the Chinese, or anyone else, insofar as that helps us understand causation. Moreover, much factual information from *within* the black community is also very revealing as to what factors do and do not promote advancement. This may well provide very little advice to those operating within the constraints set by contemporary social policy. But the real point is to have social policy better informed as to what works and what doesn't.

# CULTURE VERSUS COLOR

Once the question of the causes of the current situation of blacks can be seen as in fact a question, and not a foregone conclusion, it is possible to test alternative beliefs in a number of ways.

Blacks may "all look alike" to racists, but there are profound internal cultural differences among blacks.[17] Insofar as racism and discrimination are directed at blacks in general, the incomes and occupations of those blacks who differ culturally provide some indication of the effect of other factors—especially when and if the economic level of these subsets of blacks are comparable to those of their counterparts in the white population. In short, we can compare people of the same color and different culture, as well as people of similar culture and different color. Both comparisons provide clues to the relative weights of color and culture.

## West Indians

Black West Indians living in the United States are a group physically indistinguishable from black Americans, but with a cultural background that is quite different.[18] If current employer racial discrimination is the primary determinant of below-average black income, West Indians' incomes would be similarly affected. Yet West Indian family incomes are 94 percent of the U.S. national average, while the family incomes of blacks as a group are only 62 percent of the national average. West Indian "representation" in professional occupations is double that of blacks, and slightly *higher* than that of the U.S. population as a whole.[19] The argument has sometimes been made that white employers distinguish West Indians from other blacks by accent, birthplace, or place of schooling and that this differentiation in their treatment explains the substantial intergroup economic differences between these two sets of blacks in the same economy. Again, the test is not plausibility but evidence. If accent, birthplace or place of schooling are responsible for West Indians' advantages in the marketplace, then those West Indians lacking such obvious clues for American employers would not be expected to have comparable advantages over other blacks. *Second-generation* West Indians—born in the United States of West Indian parents—are less likely to have an accent and would have no distinguishing place of birth or schooling.

If employer discrimination explains the economic condition of blacks as well as the different conditions of West Indians, then second-generation West Indians should not be expected to have as large an advantage over other blacks. If, on the other hand, West Indian advantages are cultural, then second-generation West Indians might be expected to have even *more* advantages over other blacks, since they continue to benefit from the values and behavior patterns of their parents, plus whatever additional benefits derive from their parents' socioeconomic success and their own greater familiarity with American society. In short, diametrically opposite predictions regarding second-generation West Indians derive from the theory of cultural differences and the theory of employer discrimination as explanations of black incomes below the national average.

The facts about the economic conditions of second-generation West Indians are rather dramatic in themselves, and decisive in their implications. Second-generation West Indians have even higher incomes than the first-generation West Indians, and higher incomes than the national average—or the incomes of Anglo-Saxons. Second-generation West Indians also have higher proportions in the professions than other blacks, first-generation West Indians, the national average, or Anglo-Saxons.[20] These data are from the 1970 census, which is to say, they are 1969 incomes— two years before the 1971 federal guidelines mandating quota hiring, and so cannot be explained as effects of affirmative action.

Nor is this simply a matter of one group's starting out ahead of another. Census data also show that it takes the average West Indian immigrant eleven years to overtake native-born blacks in income.[21] This fact also undermines the notion that employer favoritism explains West Indian advantages over native blacks. It is, incidentally, a common pattern among immigrants to eventually overtake native-born people of the same ancestry.[22] There are various possible reasons for this, the most likely being selective migration.[23] But the point here is not to praise, blame, grade or morally rank groups of human beings. The purpose is to try to understand what factors do and do not prove decisive in economic advancement, regardless of what is commonly believed.

## Home and Family

Blacks and whites are not just people with different skin colors. Nor is a history of slavery the only difference between them. Like many other groups in contemporary America—and around the world and down through history —blacks and whites have different cultures that affect how they live individually and collectively. At the same time, there is sufficient overlap that some sets of blacks have a home life and family pattern very similar to those of most whites. Insofar as color is the over-riding factor in economic position, this will make relatively little difference in the incomes of such sets of blacks. Insofar as such cultural factors reflect traits that prove valuable and decisive in the marketplace, such sets of blacks should have incomes comparable to those of whites. Once more, opposite effects would be expected, according to which premise is correct.

A comparison of black and white male youths in 1969—again, before affirmative action—throws light on the role of color and culture. Harvard economist Richard Freeman compared blacks and whites whose homes included newspapers, magazines, and library cards, and who had also gone on to obtain the same number of years of schooling. There was no difference in the average income of these whites compared to these blacks.[24] This had not always been true. In earlier periods, such cultural factors had little weight.[25] But by 1969 it was true—during "equal opportunity" policies and before "affirmative action."

Home and family life differ in other ways between blacks and whites. Husband-wife families are more prevalent among whites than among blacks, though declining over time among both groups. About half of all black families with children are one-parent families, while more than four-fifths of all white families with children are two-parent families.[26] But what of those black families that are two-parent families—more like the white families in this respect and perhaps in other respects as well? To the extent that racial discrimination is the crucial factor in depressing black income, there should be little difference between the incomes of these black families relative to their white counterparts than there is between the incomes of blacks and whites as a whole. But insofar as family structure reflects cultural values in general, those blacks whose family structure reflects more general norms of behavior should be more fortunate in the job market as well.

For more than a decade, young black husband-wife families outside the South have had incomes virtually identical to those of young white husband-wife families outside the South.[27] In some years black families of this description

80

have had incomes a few percentage points higher than their white counterparts. Today, where husbands and wives are both college-educated, and both working, black families of this description earn slightly *more* than white families of this description—nationwide and without regard to age.[28]

The implication of all this is not, of course, that blacks as a group are doing as well as whites as a group—or are even close to doing as well. On the contrary. The average income of blacks as a group remains far behind the average income of whites as a group. What we are trying to find out is the extent to which this is due to cultural differences rather than color differences that call forth racism and discrimination.

A racist employer is hardly going to squelch his racism when he learns that a given black worker is under 35, married, and living outside the South. Nor is he likely to put aside his racism because he knows that both husband and wife are college educated. All that such demographic characteristics indicate is that these particular sets of blacks are culturally atypical of blacks in general. The question is whether that makes any real difference in the marketplace, given that they are still black and are competing with whites with similar cultural advantages, as well as advantages of color. According to the civil rights vision, it doesn't make any great difference but according to the empirical evidence, it makes an enormous difference. It even produces parity of income.

It would be comic, if it were not tragic, how much effort has gone into trying to discredit such data. It has been argued, for example, that black wives are more likely to work, or to work full-time, compared to white wives. This is quite true, and if all one is interested in is dismissing uncomfortable evidence, this may be as good a way as any. But if one is serious, then the next logical question is: What happens when *both* black and white couples work full-time, year around? The answer is that the young black couples outside the South still make as much as the white couples of the same description.[29]

# STRENGTHS AND WEAKNESSES OF BLACKS

The social pathology of blacks is too well known to require elaboration—high rates of crime and family desertion, and low rates of school completion, head a list that is all too familiar. What has received relatively little attention are the factors producing economic advancement among blacks. Indeed, as the discussion of husband-wife families indicated, there is a positive hostility to analyses of black success, when these cut across the grain of the civil rights vision. Nevertheless, it is useful to consider those things that have, over the years, raised black income, both absolutely and relative to white income.

Prior to World War II, black family income averaged less than half that of whites.[30] From 1940 to 1960 the principal factor that raised black income, both absolutely and relative to white income, was migration—from low-income areas to higher-income areas.[31] The great migrations of blacks out of the South—comparable in magnitude to the historic international migrations of emigrants from Europe—were among the key factors in black economic advancement. It should be noted that when these migrations began back before the *First* World War, the black leaders of that time generally opposed them. Neither W.E.B. DuBois nor Booker T. Washington, nor most of their colleagues or disciples, was in favor of these mass migrations. But blacks made their own individual decisions. They neither cast down their buckets where they were nor spent much energy trying to change southern whites. History suggests that they were right and their leaders wrong.

Blacks' improvements in education have been almost an untold story. It must be remembered that blacks were almost totally destitute of the most elementary literacy when slavery ended, a little over a hundred years ago. Most could neither read nor write their own names. To go from this point to where most blacks were at least literate, and to do it in half a century after emancipation was indeed "an accomplishment seldom witnessed in human history,"[32] as a distinguished economic historian has noted. The painful effort that this took in virtually impossible circumstances remains largely ignored to this day, though research has been published and is gathering dust on the shelves. More recent studies of successful black schools,[33] or of the successful education of blacks in white Catholic schools,[34] for example, have seldom aroused much interest or support from civil rights groups. More usually, such success has aroused resentment and anger from believers in the civil rights vision, for most of these successes were produced in ways that had little to do with the civil rights vision—and often in ways that contradicted its premises.

When the U.S. Supreme Court declared in 1954 that separate schools were inherently inferior, within walking distance of that Court was an all-black public school whose performance had equaled or surpassed that of white schools in the District of Columbia for more than 80 years.[35] NAACP attorney Thurgood Marshall had come from a similar school in Baltimore.[36] Most of the things that social reformers promote as "prerequisites" for good education today seldom existed in these or other outstanding black schools—nor outstanding schools for Jews, Chinese, or Japanese youngsters.[37]

Anyone who has been privileged to live through the past generation of changes among blacks knows that there have been many changes that cannot be quantified. One need only listen to an interview with a Bill Russell or an O. J. Simpson, or many other articulate black athletes today, and compare that with interviews with black athletes of a generation ago, to appreciate just one symptom of a profound transformation that has affected a wide segment of the black population.

It may be understandable that black politicians and civil rights organizations would want to claim the lion's share of the credit for the economic improvements that black people have experienced. But despite their constant attempts to emphasize the role of the demand side of the equation, and particularly discrimination and anti-discrimination laws, the fact is that enormous changes were taking place on the supply side. Blacks were becoming a different people. More were acquiring not only literacy but higher levels of education, skills, and broader cultural exposure. The advancement of blacks was not simply a matter of whites letting down barriers.

Much has been made of the fact that the numbers of blacks in high-level occupations increased in the years following passage of the Civil Rights Act of 1964. But the number of blacks in professional, technical, and other high-level occupations more than doubled in the decade *preceding* the Civil Rights Act of 1964.[38] In other occupations, gains by blacks were greater during the 1940s—when there was practically no civil rights legislation—than during the 1950s.[39] In various skilled trades, the income of blacks relative to whites more than doubled between 1936 and 1959.[40] The trend was already under way. It may well be that both the economic and the legal advances were products of powerful social transformations taking place in the black population and beginning to make themselves felt in the consciousness of whites, as well as in the competition of the marketplace.

Knowledge of the strengths of blacks has been ignored or repressed in a different way as well. Few people today are aware that the ghettos in many cities were far safer

84

places two generations ago than they are today, both for blacks and for whites. Incredulity often greets stories by older blacks as to their habit of sleeping out on fire escapes or on rooftops or in public parks on hot summer nights. Many of those same people would not dare to walk through those same parks today in broad daylight. In the 1930s whites went regularly to Harlem at night, stayed until the wee hours of the morning, and then stood on the streets to hail cabs to take them home.[41] Today, not only would very few whites dare to do this, very few cabs would dare to be cruising ghetto streets in the wee hours of the morning.

Why should discussion of positive achievements by blacks ever be a source of embarrassment, much less resentment, on the part of black leaders? Because many of these positive achievements occurred in ways that completely undermine the civil rights vision. If crime is a product of poverty and discrimination as they say endlessly, why was there so much less of it when poverty and discrimination were much worse than today? If massive programs are the only hope to reduce violence in the ghetto, why was there so much less violence long before anyone ever thought of these programs? Perhaps more to the point, have the philosophies and policies so much supported by black leaders contributed to the decline in community and personal standards, and in family responsibility, so painfully visible today? For many, it may be easier to ignore past achievements than to face their implications for current issues.

The negative features of black life may be far more politically usable, as in the "long hot summer" of violence that is routinely predicted each spring if various political demands are not met. However, the long-run implications of constantly talking as if welfare mothers, drug addicts, and street hoodlums were typical of the black population is that it may be forgotten by the larger society that most black adults are people who work and pay taxes like everyone else. Together with such chronic irritants as affirmative action and busing, this raises serious questions about the long-run prognosis for race relations in the United States.

# EARMARKED BENEFITS AND CONCEALED LOSSES

Particular laws and social policies may benefit or harm blacks directly as blacks or indirectly as members of the general society. The magnitude of the benefit or harm is not determined by whether blacks or minorities are specified, or even thought of, when the laws or policies are instituted. Politically, however, it makes an enormous difference whether benefits are earmarked. Black politicians and civil rights leaders obviously gain when they can deliver benefits earmarked for their constituency. Resentment in the white community—and sometimes other minority communities—is likewise heightened when particular laws, programs or policies are publicly labeled as benefits for blacks.

Benefits that blacks receive as members of the general society produce neither the same political gain for black leaders nor build up the same resentments in the white population. No doubt the G.I. Bill after World War II had an almost revolutionary effect on the ability of blacks to attend college, but it produced neither racial strife nor political breast-beating by black leaders.

Similar principles apply to harm that is done to blacks. Even the most trivial, explicitly racial, restriction will provoke resentments that can easily lead to fervent crusades. But substantial, pervasive, and enduring harm may be done to blacks as part of the general society without arousing even passing interest. For example, numerous empirical studies by economists over the past few decades have repeatedly concluded that minimum wage laws have their most devastating impact on black teenagers,[42] whose unemployment rates have soared, but black political and civil rights leaders have remained unconcerned and have continued to support such laws, which are vital to the labor unions who are the political allies of the black leadership.

Because blacks are a minority, black leaders can accomplish little or nothing without political allies—and the *quid pro quo* is the essence of politics. To get support for earmarked benefits for blacks, it is necessary to support other benefits for the allies' constituents. These benefits for other constituencies may be harmful to blacks, but such harm may not even be noticed politically, much less measured.

Subsidies to farmers raise food prices (as well as taxes and inflationary deficits) but the effect of this on blacks is not a racial issue in the political arena. Food stamps are. Yet the question whether blacks have lost more through the agricultural subsidy program than they have gained through food stamps does not even arise politically. Black politicians are therefore free to vote for agricultural subsidies in exchange for farm state Congressmen's votes for food stamps. The benefits are earmarked and the losses concealed. Whether blacks are better off or worse off on net balance is another question entirely. Most blacks—72 percent[43]—receive *no* food stamps, so for them this whole logrolling operation has produced a complete loss.

A recent book entitled *The State Against Blacks,* by Professor Walter E. Williams, details the catastrophic racial impact of various occupational licensing laws, which have had the net effect of forcing blacks out of many well-paying occupations where they were once well represented. Yet this factual study, well buttressed with official statistics, has aroused no response from black political and civil rights leaders, to whom Williams is anathema.

Taxi licensing laws, for example, have enormous racial impact. In almost all major American cities, the number of taxi licenses is restricted,[44] regardless of how many qualified people want to drive cabs. These artificial limitations drive up the market price of the license—to $20,000 in Philadelphia and $60,000 in New York[45]—and thereby puts it beyond the reach of most blacks or other lower-income groups. Philadelphia has a grand total of 14 licensed black cab drivers[46] in a city of nearly 1,500 licensed taxis. By contrast, about 70 percent of the 10,000 taxis in Washington, D.C., are driven by blacks. Washington is one of the exceptional cities *without* restrictive licensing. The net result is that (1) the racial composition of taxi drivers is radically different, and (2) the total number of jobs as taxi drivers is several times as large as in Philadelphia, even though Philadelphia has a larger population than Washington.

Politically, however, it makes far more sense for a black leader to fight tooth and nail for a hundred more CETA jobs in the Philadelphia ghetto than to fight for an end to taxi licensing restrictions, even though the latter would probably mean thousands more jobs for blacks—jobs with far higher pay than CETA jobs and of permanent duration. Ghetto jobs are an earmarked benefit, however few, tenuous and low paid. Benefits to blacks as members of the general public are no feather in a black leader's cap, even if blacks are benefited more than others by gaining access that was nearly impossible for them before.

Not only licensing laws but federal regulation and unionization have forced blacks out of many well-paying fields. In the federally regulated interstate trucking business, for example, less than one percent of the required Interstate Commerce Commission (I.C.C.) authorization certificates are held by blacks.[47] Here, as in the case of restrictive taxi

88

licensing, there is no real question as to whether there are any "qualified" blacks available. But a nationwide I.C.C. authorization certificate, which would cost in the millions to purchase in the marketplace from an existing carrier, is held by only one black trucker.[48]

In the railroad industry, the combination of regulation and unionization has proven catastrophic for blacks. In 1910, one-fourth of all locomotive firemen in the South were black. By 1960 that was down to 7 percent. This also sheds further light on the role of racism. In the South, where racism has been strongest, blacks remained better represented in the railroad industry (as well as the construction industry and other well-paid occupations) longer than in the North, because the South was more resistant to unionization. Blacks in the midwest, northeast or far west were never even 2 percent of the locomotive firemen in those regions.[49]

Unionization drove out blacks in two ways: (1) directly through discriminatory rules and policies, and (2) indirectly, by artificially raising the wage rates and making them uniform. Artificially high wage rates create a chronic surplus of job applicants, making discrimination less costly. Uniform rates eliminate any incentive an employer might have to hire a black worker who might be available for less than a white worker, especially if the black worker had less experience, skill or other qualifications. Unionization, like minimum wage laws, protect those who are already established on the inside, at the expense of those on the outside. In the construction industry, unionized contractors are aided by the Davis-Bacon Act, which requires that "prevailing wages"—in practice, union wages—be paid by contractors who do work for the government. This makes it virtually impossible for non-union contractors to get the vast amount of business coming from the government. Most minority contractors are non-union.[50]

There are virtually endless examples of concealed losses to blacks that evoke no political response from black leaders. Earmarked benefits are what pay off for these leaders politically, however small or even counterproductive these earmarked programs may be for blacks. Affirmative action, as noted in Chapter 2, benefits primarily those blacks already more advantaged, making more disadvantaged blacks worse off. It is, however, an earmarked benefit, and therefore politically sacred. It is also a continuing source of resentment against blacks.

The civil rights vision and the civil rights leadership continue pushing an approach which has proved counterproductive for the mass of disadvantaged blacks, beneficial primarily to those already advantaged, and which accumulates resentments against all blacks. These resentments are increasingly expressed in hate groups like the Ku Klux Klan and the Nazis, which are gaining members not only among ignorant southern rednecks but also in more middle class and educated classes across the nation—in short, in places where they never had a foothold before. Earmarked benefits for blacks provide some of these hate groups' strongest appeals to whites, however little these earmarked policies actually help blacks, either absolutely or compared to more general social benefits that would not have the same potential for racial polarization.

## CHAPTER FIVE

# THE
# SPECIAL CASE
# OF WOMEN

Because women have historically earned lower average incomes than men, and have been less well represented in many high-level occupations, their situation has often been analogized to that of racial and ethnic minorities. But women are not only not a minority statistically (they constitute just over half the population of the United States), their incomes and occupational patterns are also quite different from those of low-income racial and ethnic groups. One of the similarities, however, is that a whole constellation of beliefs about the history and current economic role of women has arisen—a vision that has largely insulated itself from facts.

## BELIEFS VERSUS FACTS

The familiar explanation of sex differences in incomes and occupational representation is that male employers discriminate against female employees. The persistence of the same patterns after discrimination was outlawed has been seen as merely showing how determined employers are to persist in discriminatory behavior.

## The "59 Percent" Cliché

The median annual income of women has generally fluctuated in recent years at a level just under three-fifths of that of men. From this statistic has derived the non sequitur that a woman is paid just 59 percent of what a man receives *for doing the same work*. This number has been repeated innumerable times throughout the media, with appropriate expressions of moral outrage—but without scrutiny as to its validity. In reality, women work substantially fewer hours annually than men,[1] in part because a much higher proportion of women are *part-time* workers.[2] Women also average fewer continuous years of employment on a given job.[3] Most of these differences relate to marriage and motherhood. The relevant question, as far as the issue of employer discrimination is concerned, is: What of those women to whom marriage and motherhood do not apply, the women who remain single and work full time? For such women, an entirely different picture emerges.

Women who remain single earn 91 percent of the income of men who remain single, in the age bracket from 25 to 64 years old.[4] Nor can the other 9 percent automatically be attributed to employer discrimination, since women are typically not educated as often in such highly paid fields as mathematics, science, and engineering, nor attracted to physically taxing and well-paid fields such as construction work, lumberjacking, coal mining, and the like. Moreover, the rise of unwed motherhood means that even among women who never married, the economic constraints of motherhood have not been entirely eliminated.

This virtual parity in income between men *who never marry* and women who never marry is not a new phenomenon, attributable to affirmative action. In 1971, women who had remained unmarried into their thirties and who had worked

92

continuously since high school earned slightly higher incomes than men of the very same description.[5] In the academic world, single women who received their Ph.D.'s in the 1930s had by the 1950s become full professors slightly *more* often than male Ph.D.'s as a whole.[6] Academic women who never married averaged slightly *higher* incomes in 1968–69 than academic men who never married—all this before affirmative action quotas.[7]

How, then, can women as a group be so far behind men as a group, in both incomes and occupations? Because most women become wives and mothers—and the economic results are totally different from a man's becoming a husband and father. However parallel these roles may be verbally, they are vastly different in behavioral consequences. There are reasons why there are no homes for unwed fathers.

The economic ramifications of marriage and parenthood are profound, and often directly opposite in their effects on men and women. Marriage increases a man's rate of participation in the labor force compared to single men and reduces a woman's labor force participation rate compared to single women.[8] A married man's hours worked annually increase with the number of children. A married woman's hours decrease as the number of children increase.[9] Married men work more and earn more than single men, while it is just the reverse with women. Married men with children work the most and earn the most, while married women with children work the least and earn the least. Altogether, married women living with their husbands average only 25 percent of the annual income of married men living with their wives.[10] The big difference is not between men and women, but between married women and everyone else.

The very choice of occupation, and of education for an occupation, is dominated by the likelihood of a career interruption for a woman, due to marriage and motherhood. In some fields, just a few years' absence renders much of one's skill and knowledge obsolete. In other fields, the skill or aptitude in question is just as valuable after several years away as it was before. For example, a physicist loses about half the value of his or her knowledge from a six-year layoff, but it would take an historian more than a quarter of a century to suffer a similar loss.[11] There are many different occupations scattered across a wide spectrum of obsolescence rates.[12] Women have historically specialized in fields that they could leave and re-enter some years later, without large losses from obsolescence.

Someone who is a good editor, teacher, or librarian today is likely to be good in these occupations again in five or six years. But a tax attorney who has missed five or six years of tax legislation and its judicial interpretation cannot advise a client as effectively as someone who has been keeping up with these changes on a day-to-day basis. Nor can an aeronautical engineer who has missed the development of the latest jet engines, or a medical researcher who has missed the research findings and advances in techniques of the past several years. Women's occupational choices are not at all surprising, given the time and energy consumed by domestic responsibilities and the rearing of children. The traditional division of these responsibilities between men and women may be questioned, but that is wholly different from saying that differences in annual income prove widespread employer discrimination.

Part-time workers earn less total income than full-time workers, and women are more likely than men to be part-time workers—and, indeed, to choose jobs with the specific hours that allow them to be home at the particular times they consider more important.[13] This obviously limits their choice of work and prevents their maximizing even the hourly rate of pay otherwise possible.

Because of domestic responsibilities and the rearing of children, women also tend to drop out of the labor force completely more often than men do. When a woman whose children are grown re-enters the labor force, she obviously re-enters with less experience or seniority than a man of the same age who has been working continuously and full time. This too reduces the likelihood that she will earn as much per hour, be retained as often during layoffs, or promoted as rapidly.

These mundane, commonsense facts would not need to be elaborated, were it not that the civil rights vision of the world unfolds an entirely different scenario—a more dramatic and morally charged scenario that makes for more excitement in the media and a more heroic role for various rescuers and protesters. In the civil rights vision, it is employer bias and "stereotypes" that cause women as a group to have lower annual incomes than men as a group. Nor can the issue be reduced to one of mere plausibility or of selected anecdotes. Different empirical conclusions follow from different visions, and those conclusions can be checked against facts.

If sex differences in income reflect primarily employer sex bias, it would be hard to explain why that sex difference should be 9 percent in the case of women who never married and 75 percent in the case of married women living with their husbands. It would be even more difficult to explain why this sex bias should be far stronger in some fields than others—for decade after decade, despite a complete turnover of employers with the passing generations. Moreover, if the civil rights vision is correct, it is a mere coincidence that those fields whose "male chauvinism" is strongest (as evidenced by historic under-representation of women) tend to be fields where continuous full-time work is more essential—engineering rather than the humanities, research rather than teaching, law rather than publishing, sports rather than entertainment, and on and on down the list.

The central "59 percent" cliché would require us to believe that employers could survive in a competitive market, paying nearly 70 percent more for given labor than they have to, whenever that labor is male. Even if employers were that needlessly generous to men, or so consumed by ideology, waste of this magnitude would be economically fatal to those businessmen who happened to have more men on the payroll than their competitors. Far smaller differences in cost have sent innumerable businesses into bankruptcies. As in so many other areas, the civil rights vision is so preoccupied with individual *intentions* that it ignores *systemic* effects.

A more fundamental misconception underlies much discussion of the economic condition of women. Men and women cannot be compared as if they were abstract categories, in isolation from their actual behavior, particularly in marriage. Marriage is a joint venture in economic terms as it is in other terms. Married men consistently earn higher incomes than single men. One reason is that they have wives who take care of many aspects of their lives that would otherwise absorb time and energy and limit their choices of their best job opportunities.[14] In short, marriage as actually practiced often increases a man's economic options, whether he is explicitly aware of it or not.

The income earned is a joint income in origin, as well as in its use. Researchers who take literally statistics based on the fact that the man's name alone appears on his paycheck set the stage for much misunderstanding of social reality. When the husband is affluent, the wife is not poor, even if her income is only 25 percent of his—or even zero percent of his. Indeed, she is even less likely to be poor in the latter case. Whether there is justice or injustice in the disposition of family money—and in whose favor—cannot be told from income statistics, however frustrating that may be for those who scan the horizon for injustices. Nor can the income statistics deriving from these domestic arrangements prove employer discrimination at the work place.

For the very same reasons that marriage increases the husband's ability to earn money in his own name, so it decreases the wife's options for earning money in her own name. Even when both are working full time in the same field, the woman tends to do more than half the domestic chores and to select her job and interrupt her career in response to her husband's—or children's—needs far more so than the man does. The physical consequences of pregnancy and childbirth alone are enough to limit a woman's economic options. Given that inherent set of limitations, making the man the family's cash-maximizer is not a wholly irrational decision, even if it is not necessarily the best in all respects for all people. Once again, the statistical data available to third-party observers can at best only indicate the factors at work, not permit a conclusion as to whether the trade-offs chosen are best in either an efficiency sense or a moral sense for those concerned. Childbearing is not merely a deplorable cost or a loss to be shared. Children have both benefits and costs, and how each is shared cannot be determined by how much of a family's income is recorded in the official statistics under the husband's name. That does not even determine who formally spends the money, much less in whose individual or collective interest it is spent.

The effect of marriage or motherhood on a woman's job performance may be difficult for statisticians to quantify— which is not to say that there is no difference, nor that her employer sees no difference, whether or not he even knows that she is married or has children. But if she is not as willing to work overtime as often as some other work-ers (male or female), or needs more time off for personal emergencies, then that may make her less valuable as an employee or less promotable to jobs with heavier responsibilities. In some areas it is possible to quantify important aspects of job performance, however. For example, among academics, research and publication are important criteria for professional advancement. Women academics publish much less than male academics—and this has been particularly true of married women, especially those with children.[15]

Here, as elsewhere, the power of the civil rights vision is best illustrated not by the evidence marshaled in its favor but by the subordination of evidence to belief. For example, the U.S. Department of Labor has ceased to publish job turnover rates by sex since 1968.[16] When such data were published, they showed a higher turnover rate among women than men, and particularly voluntary resignations. Such inconvenient facts are now simply buried. In a similar vein, many statistical studies include as "single," women who were formerly married but are now widowed, separated or divorced. This means that economic disadvantages caused by marriage are attributed instead to employer discrimination.

Even otherwise sophisticated statistical studies often attempt to measure discrimination by projecting what women's income would be in a non-discriminatory world by statistically estimating what men of various characteristics make. But where one of these characteristics is marriage, this commits the gross fallacy of ignoring the fact that marriage has *opposite* effects on the incomes of men and women, just as it has opposite effects on their job behavior and performance. It makes sense to compare blacks and whites with the same education, for example, because more education increases the income of both. But to compare women and men on a variable that has *opposite* effects on their respective incomes is to mindlessly extend the "minority" model to women.

98

While statistics that might undermine the civil rights vision tend to be ignored or suppressed—job turnover rates, for example—any statistic that can be used to buttress that vision is likely to be pressed into service, with little regard for what is behind the numbers. For example, much is made of the fact that "female-headed families" have lower incomes than "male-headed families." But many so-called "male-headed families" are simply husband-wife families. It is hardly surprising that families with two adults earn more than families with one adult. Moreover, even broken families headed by a man average more adults than broken families headed by a woman. Moreover, they have fewer children to inhibit the employment of those adults.[17]

## History

"Before" and "after" statistics are often used to show how the number of women in high-level positions has increased since recent legislation, policy changes, or "the women's movement." From this follows the familiar conclusion that these are the *causes* of the rise of women. *Post hoc, ergo propter hoc.* Such reasoning is even more misleading in the case of women than in the case of racial and ethnic minorities, for women were often better represented in some high-level fields decades ago (or even generations ago) than they were when the women's movement or the civil rights movement began—and both their fall and later rise have been highly correlated with demographic rather than political trends.

In 1902, the proportion of people listed in *Who's Who* who were women was more than double the proportion in 1958.[18] Nearly 17 percent of all doctorates were received by women in 1921 and again in 1932, but by the late 1950s and early 1960s this was down to 10 percent. In the leading biological sciences, women's share of doctorates declined from roughly one-fourth to one-fifth in the 1930s to one-eighth by the late 1950s. In mathematics, the drop was from 15 percent to 5 percent, in economics from 10 percent to 2 percent.[19] Similar declines in women's share of doctoral degrees from the 1930s to the 1950s occurred in the humanities, law, and chemistry. The proportion of people in professional and technical occupations who were women *declined* by 9 percent from 1940 to 1950 and by an additional 9 percent from 1950 to 1968.[20] Somewhat similar trends occurred in the Soviet Union during the same years.[21] Then in the 1960s, the proportion of doctorates received by women began to turn up again, rising from 11 percent in 1960 to nearly 14 percent in 1970.[22] In short, after several years of "women's liberation," laws and lawsuits, women's proportion of doctorates was *almost* up to where it had been nearly half a century earlier.

Absolute numbers of degrees have increased greatly, for both men and women, in many fields in recent years. And in a few specialties women's proportions may have risen beyond any previous levels. But by and large, across a wide range of fields, women are simply moving back toward the proportions they achieved decades ago. Dramatic statistical changes, in absolute numbers of degrees or in proportions over a limited number of years or fields does not change this basic pattern.

Demographic trends are far more highly correlated with this historical fall and rise of women's occupational status than is any political or legal trend. The birth rate per 1,000 women was generally declining from at least the middle of the nineteenth century until the 1930s—the low point in birth rates that coincided with the high point of women's "representation" percentage in a number of high-level occupations, as already noted. But from the mid-1930s to the mid-1950s, the birth rate was generally rising.[23] These were also the years when the statistical representation of women in high-level positions began declining. If this could be attributed to rising male chauvinism, it would be hard to explain why similar employment patterns existed during the same years in women's colleges, run by women administrators.[24]

When the birth rate began to decline again, in the 1960s,[25] women's representation in high-level occupations also began to rise. Thus, historical statistics tell the same story as an examination of contemporary data—that marriage and motherhood are the major factors in the occupational status of women relative to men.

The increase in the general participation of women in the labor force at all levels has even less correlation with civil rights or the "women's liberation" movement. The rising labor force participation rates of women in general, and of working mothers in particular, goes back at least as far as 1940.[26] Nor has the rate of increase accelerated from 1960 to 1970, compared to its increase from 1950 to 1960—even though the decade of the 1960s marked the rise of "women's liberation" as well as the civil rights revolution. On the contrary, the 1950–1960 increase was slightly greater—and that from 1940 to 1950 much higher still.[27] Whatever caused this long-range trend obviously began decades before "women's liberation" or the civil rights revolution. Nor have these latter events even accelerated the pre-existing trends. They have simply appropriated the credit by sheer repetition of their vision, ignoring hard facts to the contrary.

Demographic and social trends also help explain why black women have fared better, relative to their white counterparts, than have black men relative to white men. Black women have historically participated in the labor force more so than white women, even when married and even when there were small children.[28] As early as 1950, black female college graduates earned 91 percent of the income of white female college graduates, and by 1960 were earning 2 percent more.[29] Even when black and white women

101

in general hold the same job currently, black women average more continuous experience on a given job—38 percent more.[30] The average white male remains continuously employed 77 percent longer than the average white female.[31] Nor can this be readily attributed to employer bias against women. Women voluntarily quit more frequently than men.[32]

In short, here again ordinary labor market considerations seem to explain pay differentials better than the civil rights vision. Indeed, the ability of black women to overtake white women in the marketplace is a very serious embarrassment to the civil rights vision. Believers in that vision have either ignored these data—economist Walter Williams calls it one of the best kept secrets of all time[33]—or else have resorted to *ad hoc* theories to reconcile the data with the central vision. The problem with *ad hoc* theories after the fact is that they can explain anything, and therefore can explain nothing.

# THE "EQUAL RIGHTS" AMENDMENT

It is very doubtful if any significant proportion of Americans would disagree with the literal words that introduce the Equal Rights Amendment:

> Equality of rights under the law shall not be denied or abridged by the United States or by any State on account of sex.

Indeed, these words do little more than rephrase the Fourteenth Amendment's "equal protection" clause, which applies to "persons," not men alone. Why then the bitter controversy, the ruthless political maneuvering on both sides, and finally the defeat of the Amendment? One constitutional scholar attributes the difficulties of ERA to the Amendment's having received "too much attention,"[34] to the "timidity and fear" that surrounded it.[35] A strong proponent of ERA felt impelled to be more specific, to declare that it was "not a 'unisex' amendment." She added: "The Amendment does not command similarity in result, parity, or proportional representation."[36] This goes to the heart of the issue—and of the opposition to ERA.

Many who agree with the general principle of the Amendment have been burned too often and too badly with other civil rights legislation to accept at face value the talk of equal "rights"—when in fact that concept has been repeatedly transformed to an equal *results* policy in practice. It might be argued that there was "almost nothing in the legislative history that speaks to any group rights concept,"[37] but the same could be said even more emphatically of the Civil Rights Act of 1964, which led to quotas. One might well claim that this kind of twisting of the Equal Rights Amendment would require "a rigidity of construction wholly indifferent to considerations of common sense."[38] Yet something more than abstract suspiciousness or timidity is involved, and the specific denials pinpoint precisely what has already happened repeatedly—individual rights being interpreted as group results.

The vision behind the ERA is very much the same as the vision behind other civil rights legislation and policies: "The equal status and dignity of men and women under the law is the animating purpose of the proposed Equal Rights Amendment (ERA)."[39] Because the proponents of ERA emphasize the *equality* of status between the sexes, they often assume that opponents believe in inequality. But for many opponents the crucial word is "status," not "equality." ERA, like the civil rights vision in general, focuses on status rather than *behavior*.

103

Those who believe that people should be free to make decisions on the basis of behavior fight attempts to turn all questions into status questions. When women differ from men in life expectancy, continuity of employment, physical strength, and job skills, among other behavioral differences, to view legal, economic, and other differences as status issues of constitutional dimensions is to unleash judges and bureaucrats who have wreaked havoc in other areas. Even without ERA, courts have already intervened to undo major economic commitments in pension plans because these pensions took account of the behavioral reality that women live longer than men. Given that reality, men and women can either receive equal amounts over a lifetime or equal amounts per month—but *not* both.

There is no real issue as to whether women shall be paid equally. The issue is: *Over what span of time* shall they be paid equally? Courts have imposed short-run equality even though those whose own money was involved chose long-run equality. Moreover, those who made that choice were not merely said to have chosen the wrong policy but to have violated the law and to be liable to punishment.

# EFFECTS VERSUS INTENTIONS

With women, as with racial and ethnic minorities, the effects of policies must be carefully separated from the intentions of those policies. The crucial question is not the desirability of the professed goal but the incentives and constraints created—and what they are most likely to lead to.

The imposition of monthly equality in pensions, rather than lifetime equality, has the net effect of making pension plans more expensive, the more female employees there are. Viewed as prospective behavioral incentives, rather than as a retrospective status pronouncement, this means that employers will find it more costly to hire female workers with a given pension plan and more costly to institute a given pension plan when there are more female workers. Reducing the demand for female workers or reducing the likelihood of creating a pension plan is hardly the intention of the courts, but it can easily be the result. It is not clear that anyone is economically better off after such a symbolic ruling.

Surrounding the hiring of a female job applicant with special dangers under affirmative action if her subsequent job experience (raises, promotions, layoffs) is less favorable than her peers does nothing to enhance her probability of getting hired in the first place. Neither men nor women are uniform in their skills and they will vary individually in even the most unbiased occupation. But if men who don't work out are expendable and women who don't work out are potential court cases, then the incentives created do not match the intentions.

Much of the literature on women shows little relationship between its evidence and its conclusions. "Landmark legislation and government action prohibiting employment discrimination based on sex" is credited by a U.S. Department of Labor study with increasing the labor force participation rates of women[40]—even though the data in the very same study shows this to be a long-run trend going back at least as far as 1940.[41] Moreover, the "earnings gap between men and women continued to widen" according to the same study.[42] Similarly, a study of the academic world declares that "the women's movement and affirmative action legislation have prompted higher education institutions to take significant steps to remedy a neglect of women."[43] Yet the very same study shows only mixed results after ten years of affirmative action—more academic women but their income is the same percentage of that of academic men as it was a decade earlier, and with the women constituting a *smaller* proportion of tenured faculty than before.[44] Other data show similar results,[45] despite at least 3,000 faculty sex discrimination cases filed by the Equal Employment Opportunity Commission and 117 judicial decisions on that subject.[46] Having misstated the causes, believers in the civil rights vision have also misstated the effectiveness of their cure.

## "Comparable Worth"

One of the more remarkable doctrines to emerge in recent years is that third-party observers can determine the "real" value of particular jobs, however disparate, and therefore whether employees of "comparable worth" are in fact paid the same. Thus, for example, a senior librarian is considered to be of "comparable worth" to a senior chemist, and the fact that the chemist is paid more is taken as indicating sex discrimination, since the chemists are predominantly male and librarians predominantly female.[47]

The multiplicity of unstated assumptions behind this kind of reasoning is as much an asset in politics as it is a liability in logic. It would take pages to refute each sentence, because the implicit premises would have to be elaborated first. Even if they then collapsed of their own inconsistencies, it is not clear how many readers or listeners would have been willing to stay the course as the argument tediously unfolded. That is why it is a *politically* clever argument. Demagoguery flourishes where something can be said in a few catchy words that would take volumes to disprove.

The political appeal of the "comparable worth" argument is also enhanced by giving arbitrary subjective judgments of jobs the appearance of scientific objectivity in the form of numerical point ratings for different aspects of the work. Thus the points for librarians and chemists each add up to exactly 493 points, using "standards of training and responsibility established by the State," according to the U.S. Civil Rights Commission.[48] But quantifying something inherently arbitrary makes it no less arbitrary, however much it imitates the outward signs of "science."

There is no way to add apples and oranges to get a total of "fruit." Giving so many points per strawberry, so many for mangoes, so many for pears, etc., does nothing more than put numbers on a misconception. That there are "experts" who make a living assigning points to jobs for the civil service and others proves nothing. There are people who make an even better living selling quack medicines.

Where employment and pay decisions are made by those who actually have their own money at stake, such input factors as "training and responsibility" are by no means the only considerations. Scarcity and productivity are likely to be very important, and both vary considerably from job to job and from individual to individual—too much so to be reduced to formulas. Where pay is determined in the marketplace by demand *and* supply, what the workers want is also important. A job that is considered unpleasant or known to have less steady employment will attract fewer people, unless the pay is higher enough to compensate for the differences—as judged by those actually making the choice. A carpenter and a secretary may add up to the same number of points in the bureaucratic formulas, but the fact that one works outdoors in winter's cold or summer's heat, while the other usually works indoors in a climate-controlled environment, no doubt has something to do with how easy it is to attract and hold people in these jobs.

What are called "traditional" women's jobs are often jobs which meet other special requirements that make sense to women—slow obsolescence rates, adjustable hours, and less demand for physical strength are just a few examples. Where particular jobs are especially attractive to particular groups, those jobs are likely to have their pay held down by the competition of many applicants. The EEOC calls it "job segregation"[49]—perpetuating the confusion between externally imposed restrictions and individual choices.

The pretense of bureaucratic organizations that they can define jobs "objectively" with formulas does not stop them from having to compete for workers on the basis of supply and demand. Hence the contradiction between their assertions and their actual pay scales—and a golden opportunity for "comparable worth" claims.

In a sense, such claims are a reassuring social sign that civil rights activists, whose own employment and visibility depend upon maintaining an adequate flow of injustices, are forced to resort to things like "comparable worth" in order to keep busy. It is also virtually a lawyers' full-employment act, since it will be possible to argue interminably on both sides as to the items that go into the job point totals, which determine "comparable worth." Moreover, labor unions have every incentive to embrace this doctrine, since achieving "comparability" can only be done by raising some salaries, not by lowering others. This is especially so in government employment, since no politician wants to be on record against equality, comparability, or equity. The net result is likely to be that taxpayers will end up paying far more than necessary to get the public's work done.

Just a few years ago, "comparable worth" arguments would have been laughed away for their sheer meaninglessness. That they are taken in deadly earnest in many places —including courts—is one indication of the advantage of any argument that fits the framework of the civil rights vision.

## CHAPTER SIX

# RHETORIC OR REALITY?

Civil rights are fundamental to a free society and to human dignity. Their blatant denial to many, but especially to blacks in the South, was for too long a mockery of American ideals. Civil rights are important in and of themselves, and not as a miracle ingredient from which to expect great economic or educational changes in accordance with particular social theories. Civil rights have not "failed" or remained "illusory" because the economic or social consequences predicted by those theories have not materialized. It is, after all, possible that those theories have failed.

The battle for civil rights was fought and won—at great cost—many years ago. Like any fundamental human achievement, these rights cannot be taken for granted and must be safeguarded. But civil rights are not protected or enhanced by the growing practice of calling every issue raised by "spokesmen" for minority, female, elderly, or other groups, "civil rights" issues. The right to vote is a civil right. The right to win is not. Equal treatment does not mean equal results. Everything desirable is not a civil right. Nor are the institutions or methods that produced civil rights likely to produce all the other things required to advance minorities, women, or others.

The year 1984 is not only an anniversary for civil rights. It is also the title of George Orwell's great novel that introduced Newspeak. The reality of an historic struggle for civil rights has degenerated into the hustling rhetoric of Newspeak. "Equal opportunity" now means preferential treatment. "Voting rights" now include preferential chances to win. School desegregation no longer means the right to attend any public school, regardless of race, but being forced to attend where you are told, according to race. "Equal justice for all" now means compensatory benefits for some—usually the more fortunate of those who share the political label "disadvantaged."

These are not mere aberrations or perversities. They are inherent in the vision of the world accepted uncritically in the heady days of the civil rights revolution. In various other countries around the world, the same vision has turned "equal" into "preferential" and rights into results. In those countries as well, *the advantaged have benefited in the name of the disadvantaged.*

# PREFERENCES INTERNATIONALLY

In Uganda, the first major boycott of the Asians was organized and instigated by African businessmen who competed with Asians, and by the more educated Africans who stood to gain by replacing Asians in the civil service.[1] In various cities and localities in India, strident (and sometimes violent) demands for preferential hiring of disadvantaged locals, over migrants from other parts of India, have repeatedly been led by newly educated people seeking middle-class jobs.[2] Much the same story could be told, with local variations, of the French separatists in Quebec,[3] and preferential treatment in Thailand,[4] among others. Those who believe in the essential brotherhood of man have little reason to be surprised to see similar patterns emerging in the United States.

Nor has the effectiveness of preferences and quotas been demonstrable elsewhere.[5] The Malaysian preferential and quota system, for example, has been in operation for about as long as that in the United States, has been far more sweeping, and has been administered by Malays for Malays to reduce their economic disadvantage or under-representation vis-à-vis the Chinese minority, who have long been dominant in the economy. Before this program was instituted, the average Chinese in Malaysia made double the income of the average Malay. After a decade of this program—and stringent laws forbidding any public criticism of this or any other aspect of Malaysian racial policies—the Chinese still made double the income of the Malays.[6] The argument made by minority "spokesmen" in the United States, that affirmative action has failed for lack of government commitment or of minority power, does not apply at all in Malaysia, where Malays have overwhelming political power. Someone once said that an idea which fails repeatedly may possibly be wrong. It is by no means clear that the supporters of affirmative action are prepared to go that far. There are still many true believers to whom all evidence is irrelevant.

Many who perceive the ineffective or counterproductive aspects of preferential policies nevertheless hesitate to "go back" to the world that existed prior to the civil rights revolution. Yet that is a false choice. No one could "go back" even if he wanted to. When mandatory busing was overruled and stopped in Los Angeles, school integration continued. There are long waiting lists of people of all races for the "magnet" schools of that city. Most of the trends in minority economic and educational advancement that are used as evidence for the social effectiveness of civil rights policies began *before* such policies began and were

111

not visibly accelerated by them. The same has been true in distant Bombay.[7]

# REALITIES VERSUS PERCEPTIONS

What is ignored in much discussion of civil rights, and of intergroup relations in general, is that it is not simply a question of "perceptions" or animosities—that there is an underlying reality that cannot be talked away. Intergroup differences or the need for qualifications cannot be sneered aside as mere code words for discrimination.

What is lacking in many discussions of discrimination is a sense of economics. To say that women receive only 59 percent of what men receive for doing the same work is to say that employers pay men 70 percent more than they have to, to get a given job done. No businessman can spot his competitors that large an advantage and hope to survive in the economy. Even assuming that all employers are equally consumed by sexism and equally unconcerned about their own survival, just a small difference in male-female proportions among their employees would spell the difference between bankruptcy and soaring profits. Even racism in South Africa has not stopped the hiring of blacks over whites under such conditions—which is why massive *political* intervention in the economy has been necessary to preserve "white supremacy" there.[8] Similarly, sweeping Jim Crow *laws* were used in the South to keep blacks "in their place" precisely because of the futility of trying to do so in a competitive economy. Even at the height of southern racism, black-white pay differentials for the same job never remotely approached the kind of male-female pay differences that would exist if the "59 percent" cliché was accurate.[9]

At the height of anti-Japanese feeling in the early twen-

112

tieth-century United States, the initial practice of paying white workers more than Japanese workers collapsed—and apparently *reversed*—as it became evident that the Japanese worked harder.[10] Again, *political* intervention in the economy was necessary in California in order to try to stop the economic rise of the Japanese, precisely because economic pressures were too great to keep them down under competitive conditions.

From an economic point of view, to say that any group is systematically underpaid or systematically denied as much credit as they deserve is the same as saying that an opportunity for unusually high profit exists for anyone who will hire them or lend to them. Even if all outsiders are too blind to see this, then the more fortunate members of that group have unusually profitable opportunities as employers and lenders. When Japanese American farmers began bidding for underpaid Japanese American laborers in the early twentieth century, white farmers had no choice but to join the bidding war rather than lose good workers. Had they attempted to operate with all-white work forces, they would have spotted an enormous advantage to Japanese farmers, whom they were having difficulty enough competing against, as it was.

Similarly, the unusually large saving propensities of Italian immigrants (found in a number of countries[11]), and their reliability in repaying loans, made them exceptionally good banking customers—whether or not American bankers "perceived" this reality. *Italians* knew it. One group of Italians pooled their money to create a bank in San Francisco called the Bank of Italy, precisely to appeal to their fellow immigrants. It became so successful that eventually it grew into the largest bank in the world, under its new name—Bank of America.[12]

Economics is not merely a matter of "perceptions" but of underlying realities that are transmitted through the marketplace. To say that women and blacks are generally discriminated against in banking and credit is the same thing economically as saying that banks and other lending institutions with mostly black or female customers tend to have exceptionally profitable opportunities. But the actual history of such institutions suggests nothing of the kind.

Third-party observers from the sidelines may say grandly that it is "irrelevant" what a woman's marital status is, but if in reality a married woman with no income and an affluent husband is a better credit risk than the average single woman with a steady job, then when such women get divorced, they will find their credit ratings dropping. To say that banks that operate this way are mistaken is to say that other banks and lending institutions have unusually profitable opportunities by operating differently. Women's banks, for example, would follow a path much more like the Bank of America if they had access to such an especially profitable clientele, constituting just over half of the population of the country. In reality, however, the First Women's Bank has been a financial disaster, despite preferential treatment in handling government funds.[13] Historically, black banks have had extremely high rates of failure,[14] and those that survived generally placed more of their money outside of their communities than did white banks.[15]

The domination of civil rights discussions and decisions by lawyers and politicians—people who deal in plausibilities made persuasive by words—may help explain the ignoring of systemic processes like the economic marketplace and the ignoring of underlying realities immune to words. The attempt to reduce intergroup differences to the perceptions and biases of others implicitly assumes that these intergroup differences are not real or consequential.

# STANDARDS AND QUALIFICATIONS

Economic realities are also ignored by those who consider any standards or tests to be out of place for "unskilled" work, and any group disparities among such employees clear evidence of discrimination. But there are no occupations in which human beings are interchangeable, however simple an occupation may appear to an observer with no personal economic stake in the performance of that job. It may require little direct technical skill to pump gas but it matters ecomically to the filling station owner whether the person who pumps his gas can be depended upon to show up every day on time, so that he is not caught shorthanded and his rush-hour customers delayed to or from work—or lost to a rival filling station across the street because he has a line backed up at his pumps. It matters economically whether the attendant is pleasant and attentive or surly and forgets to check under the hood when asked. There are no jobs that "anybody" can do or where standards are out of place.

Nor can the "job-relatedness" of the standards be assessed in any mechanical way by the nature of the task. Standards that are *person*-related play the same economic role as standards that are *job*-related. If people who finished high school seem to the employer to work out better than dropouts, third parties who were not there can neither deny this assessment nor demand that it be proved to their uninformed satisfaction. It makes no difference economically whether this was because the specific task relates to what was learned in high school or because those who finish high school differ in outlook from those

115

who drop out. Neither does it matter economically whether those who score higher on certain tests make better workers because of knowing the specific items on those tests or because the kind of people who read enough to do well on tests tend to differ in outlook from those who spend their time in activities that require no reading.

To say that some employers are mistaken in their criteria is to say that other employers have special profit opportunities by hiring those workers passed over—and in a competitive market, that means that mistakes are likely to be corrected. It does *not* mean, however, that every difference in "representation" is a mistake, or that race, sex, or other group designations were used as criteria. Third-generation Mexican Americans earn 20 percent higher incomes than first-generation Mexican Americans of the same age,[16] though it is doubtful if most employers seek the genealogical information necessary to make such a distinction.

There is neither evidence nor even the pretense of evidence for the proposition that all groups are prepared to make the same sacrifices to achieve the same ends, quite aside from any question of equal capability, natural or acquired. Yet without that assumption, there is no reason to expect the even representation which is used as a norm to measure discrimination.

There is considerable evidence that in fact significant changes have occurred over the years in both cultural orientations and in group capabilities. These changing realities may have much to do with the changing perceptions that made the civil rights revolution possible. Blacks in particular have had enormous internal changes in just one century. A hundred years ago, most blacks could neither read nor write their own names, were living in the backward rural South, and were so unable to take care of themselves that

116

their mortality rates were higher than they had been under slavery.[17] What has happened in the century since then has been one of the great social transformations of a people—a transformation largely ignored by those who ascribe black advancement to political and legalistic actions. There have also been some retrogressions over the past generation, in some respects—notably crime and teenage pregnancy. Although political and legalistic activities are automatically credited with the advancement of minorities, neither is even questioned as a possible cause of the retrogressions, despite the role of "civil rights" organizations in the promotion of welfare and their role in the easing of crime control, epitomized by the NAACP Legal Defense Fund's leading role in opposing the death penalty.

# CIVIL RIGHTS VERSUS "CIVIL RIGHTS"

An attorney and former official of the NAACP Legal Defense Fund inadvertently revealed much of the evolution of that organization when he noted that by the mid-1960s "the long golden days of the civil rights movement had begun to wane," that the legal tools which it had developed "now threatened to collect dust."[18] They needed new missions—and they found them, the crusade against the death penalty being just one. But they continued to call themselves "civil rights" organizations and the media have largely repeated that designation. In reality, the crusade for civil rights ended years ago. The scramble for special privilege, for turf, and for image is what continues on today under that banner and with that rhetoric.

The possibility that "too much" would be done to benefit minorities, women, or others is the least likely of the consequences of the new conception of civil rights. There is much reason to fear the *harm* that it is currently doing to its supposed beneficiaries, and still more reason to fear the long-run consequences of polarizing the nation. Resentments do not accumulate indefinitely without consequences. Already there are signs of hate organizations growing in parts of the country and among more educated social classes than ever took them seriously before. As a distinguished writer has said in a different context: "It takes a match to start a fire but the match alone is not enough."[19] Many racial policies continually add to the pile of combustible material, which only needs the right political arsonist to set it off.

Risks must be taken for genuine civil rights. But the kinds of internal struggles that have torn other multi-ethnic societies apart must be for something more than the continuing visibility of organizations or the continued employment of their lawyers.

The dangers of the present course are both insidious and acute. Among the insidious dangers are the undermining of minority and female self-confidence by incessant reiteration of the themes of pervasive discrimination, hypocritical standards, and shadowy but malign enemies relentlessly opposing their progress. However successful this vision may be in creating a sense of dependence on "civil rights" and "women's liberation" movements, it also obscures the urgency of acquiring economically meaningful skills or developing the attitudes to apply them with the best results. Pride of achievement is also undermined by the civil rights vision that assumes credit for minority and female advancement. This makes minority and female achievement suspect in their own eyes and in the eyes of the larger society.

The more acute dangers are longer run. The spread of hate organizations may be a symptom of much more unorganized resentment among people who are still not yet prepared to join fascistic or messianic movements. The dangers of continually adding to those resentments are all the greater the more heedlessly preferential doctrines are pushed in the courts, in the federal bureaucracy and by activists.

The resentments are not only against the particular policies but also against the manner in which the law, plain honesty, and democracy itself are sacrificed on the altar of missionary self-righteousness. The covert methods by which affirmative action has been foisted on a society that rejects it, the vengeful manner in which busing has been imposed without regard for the welfare of children, and the lofty contempt of a remote and insulated elite for the mass of citizens whose feelings and interests are treated as expendable, or dismissed as mere "racism," provide the classic ingredients of blindness and hubris that have produced so many human tragedies.

However much history may be invoked in support of these policies, *no* policy can apply to history but can only apply to the present or the future. The past may be many things, but it is clearly irrevocable. Its sins can no more be purged than its achievements can be expunged. Those who suffered in centuries past are as much beyond our help as those who sinned are beyond our retribution. To dress up present-day people in the costumes and labels of history and symbolically try to undo the past is to surpass Don Quixote and jeopardize reality in the name of visions. To do so in ways that harm the already disadvantaged is to skirt the boundaries of sanity and violate the very claims of compassion used to justify it.

"Realists" who claim that preferential policies are part of a "widespread" drive for equality, and therefore "here to stay" are the most out of touch of all. Polls show no such widespread preoccupation with imposing equal results, but instead a repeated rejection of such a goal, at low- as well as high-income levels, and among blacks and women,

119

among other groups.[20] The axiomatic and passionate nature of various beliefs among contemporary intellectuals does not make those intellectuals "everybody" or those beliefs valid or inevitable. That so many act as if it does is part of the problem. No idea is "here to stay" unless we choose to accept it. History is littered with predictions of inevitability and "waves of the future."

Sincerity of purpose is not the same as honesty of procedure. Too often they are opposites. Lies and deceptions "in a good cause" are all too common, and nowhere more so than in political and legal doctrines that falsely sail under the flag of "civil rights." The perversions of the law by federal judges appointed for life have been especially brazen. While they may be personally immune to the outrage they create, neither the law nor respect for the law is immune. Courts receive unprecedentedly low ratings in polls and contempt for the law is all too apparent in all too many ways. Demoralizing a people is not a small responsibility.

Civil rights is only one of the areas in which the vision of the morally self-anointed has overridden the upholding of law or the preservation of freedom. That it has been done sincerely is not to say that it has been done honestly—or that the dishonesty has gone undetected or unresented. When judges reduce the law to a question of who has the power and whose ox is gored, they can hardly disclaim responsibility, or be morally superior, when others respond in kind. We can only hope that the response will not someday undermine our whole concept of law and freedom. Fascism has historically arisen from the utter disillusionment of the people with democratic institutions.

We are not yet at that point, and our course need never take us there, though that is the direction in which we are currently drifting. Civil rights in the original and genuine sense are still solid. The very need of organizations like the NAACP and the ACLU to find ever more remote activities

120

are evidence of that. If there is an optimistic aspect of preferential doctrines, it is that they may eventually make so many Americans so sick of hearing of group labels and percentages that the idea of judging each individual on his or her own performance may become more attractive than ever.

# THE DEGENERATION OF RACIAL CONTROVERSY

There was a time, back in the heady days of the civil rights movement, when people expected to "solve" the racial "problem"—almost as if life were an academic exercise, with answers in the back of the book. Twenty years and many disappointments later, the question is whether we can even discuss the subject rationally.

The poisonous atmosphere surrounding any attempt to debate issues involving race and ethnicity is demonstrated in many ways. In addition to the usual *ad hominem* attacks and overheated rhetoric, there has also developed a fundamental disregard for the truth, which has become widespread not only among some journalists, but is even beginning to creep into scholarly publications. Not since the days of Senator Joe McCarthy has the drive to discredit so overridden every other consideration. Lies out of whole cloth are not uncommon and straw men dot the landscape.

## SAMPLE STRAW MEN

After a decade of research, writing, and lecturing in opposition to the theory of genetic racial inferiority, including

123

CIVIL RIGHTS: RHETORIC OR REALITY?

several articles and chapters of books devoted solely to that subject,[1] I have been depicted as a *supporter* of genetic racial inferiority theories by Lem Tucker on the nationwide *CBS Morning News* and by a professor of economics in the "scholarly" *Journal of Ethnic Studies.* [2]

It can no longer be taken for granted that a reviewer or critic will even state the very subject of a book accurately. For example, *Los Angeles Times* syndicated columnist Tom Braden has attacked Walter Williams' book, *The State Against Blacks,* as a book about "affirmative action," which Braden then ringingly defends.[3] Yet affirmative action is not even mentioned in passing until page 155 of Williams' book, and a hasty reader could miss it entirely, even there. The book is about licensed occupations and government control of pay rates.

Similarly, Christopher Jencks in the *New York Review of Books* has said that my *Ethnic America* was "in effect" a book about affirmative action.[4] Phrases like "in effect" allow anything to be attributed to anybody—regardless of what he actually said. One could equally say that the dictionary is "in effect" a book about mathematics. The average dictionary in fact contains far more discussion of mathematical terms than there is discussion of affirmative action in *Ethnic America.* The book's index shows a grand total of two mentions of affirmative action, and both put together would not add up to one full page.

In a passage so phrased that a reader could easily think that it was a direct quote from me, syndicated columnist Carl Rowan expressed what was supposedly my position on my own career:

> I did all this on my own, with hard work, so I don't want government to give any lazy bastard anything.[5]

What I actually wrote about my career was:

> It would be premature at best and presumptuous at worst to attempt to draw sweeping or definitive conclusions from my personal experiences. It would be especially unwarranted to draw Horatio Alger conclusions, that perseverence and/or ability "win out" despite obstacles. The fact is, I was losing in every way until my life was changed by the Korean War, the draft, and the G.I. Bill—none of which I can take credit for. I have no false modesty about having seized the opportunity and worked to make it pay off, but there is no way to avoid the fact that there first had to be an opportunity to seize.[6]

The Rowan version was echoed by CBS correspondent Lem Tucker, who told millions of viewers of the *CBS Morning News* that my position was "that he alone, almost without bootstraps, pulled himself out of the ghetto through Harvard and the University of Chicago."[7]

It has become remarkably commonplace—and seldom commented on—to attribute positions directly the opposite of those actually taken. For example, my book *Knowledge and Decisions* argued at length that government is not a co-ordinated unit of action but "a fragmentary aggregation of decision-makers," and quoted Senator Moynihan's characterization of "the warring principalities that are sometimes known as the Federal government." Nevertheless, Lester Thurow in the *New Republic* said that it claimed that government is "a monolithic conspiracy." Having established this straw man, he could then say that this was an "angel's and devil's" theory and wisely show that the world is otherwise.[8]

125

The name of the game is showing that one's opponent is "simplistic." How it is done obviously does not matter.

Christopher Jencks' effort in this direction attacked my three-way breakdown of different kinds of discrimination. This was "too simple" according to Jencks.[9] His own breakdown? *Four* ways—apparently one-third more complex, except that his fourth kind of discrimination was one already included under one of my three. No matter. The "simplistic" theme was repeated, and repetition is a major part of such attacks. Life is of course more complex than any statement that anyone can make. What is truly simple-minded is to use this fact selectively to dismiss arguments that cannot be answered with evidence or reasons.

An almost comic example of the genesis of straw men grew out of reactions to a pair of articles of mine in the *Washington Post.* I argued that some blacks from the old elite, which denigrated and discriminated against other blacks, were now exhibiting the extreme reactions typical of reformed sinners by being blacker-than-thou. Among the examples was Patricia Roberts Harris, once a member of a sorority which refused to admit darker-skinned college girls. The uproar that followed mention of this fact— too widely known to be denied—produced the straw man that I was criticizing Mrs. Harris for being light-skinned! Mrs. Harris herself said that I was using "South African apartheid concepts of racial gradations."[10] Roger Wilkins said in *The Nation* that I was denouncing black leaders for "having light skins,"[11] while St. Clair Drake accused me of "an almost paranoid preoccupation with a non-existent 'light skin elite.' "[12] Other individuals and publications have echoed the same theme. Not one of them has given any inkling that I had criticized *behavior,* not complexion.

Others whose work has raised inconvenient questions

about race and ethnicity have encountered similar treatment. William Julius Wilson, Derrick Bell, Walter Williams and Anne Wortham come immediately to mind, but they are by no means the only targets. More important, the issue is not these particular individuals, for if distortions and character assassination were going to stop them, they would have stopped long ago. The real issue is whether the new McCarthyism creates an atmosphere in which only a handful of people dare to question publicly the prevailing vision. If it succeeds in discrediting ideas and facts it cannot answer, in intimidating others into silence, then the whole attempt to resolve urgent social issues will have to be abandoned to those with fashionable clichés and political cant—what has been aptly called "Whitespeak."

Straw men need to be examined not only in themselves, but also as indicators of what positions are too weak to defend in any other way. Many of these positions involve discrimination and policies for dealing with it.

# "REPRESENTATION" AND DISCRIMINATION

For at least twenty years, the media, politicians, the courts and intellectuals have been using numerical "representation" data to infer racial, sex, and other discrimination. The issue here is not whether any discrimination exists. The issue is whether what is used as evidence is in fact evidence. In a legal sense, the question is whether it distinguishes between the innocent and the guilty. In a larger social sense, the question is whether it clarifies or obscures the causes of very real and sometimes very large economic differences between groups.

One of many reasons why various racial and ethnic

groups are not equally represented in all occupations and institutions is that they differ greatly in their average age, as noted in Chapter 2. Those who put together straw men try to turn this into an argument that age differences alone explain virtually all racial and ethnic differences, to the complete exclusion of discrimination.

Christopher Jencks, for example, accuses me of "leaving the reader with the impression that if the median black, Indian, or Hispanic were as old as the median European, he would be almost as affluent."[13] It would be fascinating to see the actual number (and I.Q. scores) of any readers who drew that conclusion from books that repeatedly emphasized the wide range of demographic, historical, geographical, cultural, and other factors at work. In a similar vein, the U.S. Commission on Civil Rights, in a November 1982 report, depicted me as claiming that group differences result from differences in age and education and are "not a result of anything else."[14] But it is the Civil Rights Commission that has had a single, all-purpose explanation of intergroup differences—discrimination. It is precisely in opposition to this automatic inference of discrimination that such factors as age—and numerous other variables—are mentioned.

In comparing people with the same" education, to show what income differences remain as the effects of discrimination, the U. S. Commission on Civil Rights resolutely ignores vast *qualitative* differences in education that exist at every level. Black and Hispanic youngsters do not take as much mathematics in school, nor score nearly as high on standardized mathematics tests as white or Asian youngsters.[15] Similarly, black and Hispanic Ph.D.'s specialize in a vastly different mix of subjects from those in which white or Asian Ph.D.'s specialize, the former concentrating in subjects that do not require mathematics and do not pay as much. To call group differences in income between people with the "same" education, in a purely quantitative sense, "discrimination" is to play games with words.

One of the fallacies in discussions of the importance of age applies far more broadly than to age alone, and has created devastating disasters in higher education. Some ethnic groups differ little in age or income, and their small income and occupational differences may have little or nothing to do with age. From this Christopher Jencks concludes that age differences "have almost no impact on family incomes."[16]

By reasoning as Jencks does, one could also "prove" that height has no significant effect on playing basketball. Players who are six foot nine are usually about as good as players who are six foot ten. This approach would, however, leave the most blatant fact unexplained—why basketball players usually tower over the rest of us.

The same kind of reasoning has been used to "prove" that test scores have no real validity as predictors of performance in college, medical schools, etc. At a college where virtually all students score in the top ten percent on national tests, just where in that select group a particular student is located probably means much less than his motivation, emotional state, and other such personal factors. Statistical correlations between scores and results may not be very impressive *within that narrow range*. But to use this as a reason to admit students from the *bottom* half of the test scores to compete with those at the top is to set the stage for disaster.

The 1960s saw this kind of reasoning, and these kinds of disasters, on college campuses across the country. There are many today still pushing such thinking. It would be analogous to hiring midgets to play in the National Basketball Association, after having "proven" that height doesn't really matter.

# THE CASE OF THE VANISHING ASIANS

Two of the recurring themes in the literature on race and ethnicity are (1) the enormous impact of past discrimination on current incomes, and (2) the great difference between white ethnic groups, who can eventually blend into the American society, and groups marked by indelible color differences, who cannot. I have been repeatedly accused of ignoring this latter difference. But I have in fact discussed this difference in every book I have written on ethnicity—and have repeatedly found empirically that there is less there than meets the eye.

Asians disappear mysteriously from the discussions of those who make the white-nonwhite difference economically crucial. So do West Indian blacks.

A massive study by the U.S. Civil Rights Commission was typical of this approach—and of the vanishing Asians. Their 1982 report inundated the public and the media with statistical differences ("disparities" and "inequities") in the employment and income patterns of blacks, Hispanics, and women. Against this backdrop, they unfurled the usual explanations of racism and sexism. But not one speck of data on Asians appeared in this voluminous compilation—even though the explanations being offered would apply to Asians, as well as to other physically distinct minorities.

Near the end of the report, Asians were mentioned in passing, but still without any economic data. The Civil Rights Commission acknowledged that there were "discriminatory immigration laws" against Asians in the past, but was strangely reticent about acknowledging any of the other massive discriminations—not to mention violence

130

and deaths—that they suffered. The final word of the Commission's brief discussion of Asians:

> In the relatively small number of occupations in which Asians were allowed to participate they were able to attain a moderate level of economic success.[17]

In short, Asians are *confined* to such occupations as mathematicians, scientists, and engineers! By a rare coincidence, they seem to be confined to precisely the same kinds of occupations in other countries. This form of racism seems particularly odd, since the net result is that Asians, including Pacific islanders, now average ten percent higher incomes than whites, according to the 1980 Census. If this is only "moderate" success, whites must be failures.

# BOOTSTRAPS AND BLAME

One of the recurring themes in attempts to discredit critics of the welfare state is that they would leave the disadvantaged to lift themselves by their own bootstraps. "Bootstraps" is one of the classic straw man words of our time —a word used *only* to describe someone *else's* philosophy. No one has advocated it but everyone is sure that someone else has. It is symptomatic of a broader misconception that automatically translates statements of causation into statements of advice to the disadvantaged or moral statements of "blame" for the "victim."

Various publications have referred to the advice supposedly offered to the disadvantaged in *Ethnic America*—but none could ever quote any of it. There is a reason: There is no such advice there. Partly that is because so many decisions have been taken out of people's hands by the government.

Nevertheless, I am depicted as saying that blacks should be following the path of the Jews—or the Irish, the Chinese, or others, according to taste. Yet this would be strange advice indeed after my pointing out repeatedly how many of the options of former times have been destroyed by government policy. Walter Williams' book, *The State Against Blacks,* is built precisely around that theme. Yet he too is often accused of offering the same advice.

The confusion between analysis and advice has become enshrined in media thinking. One of many clever journalistic devices is to ask: "But what would you say to the welfare mother, the unemployed black teenager, the disadvantaged Hispanic?" One may as well ask a medical researcher: "But what would you say to the mother whose child is dying of leukemia?" The purpose of cause-and-effect analysis is not to offer advice or consolation to people in impossible situations, but to attempt to reduce the occurrence of such situations.

Whatever advice I have offered on public policy has almost invariably been directed toward policy makers. This advice has ranged from deregulation to education vouchers to repeal of minimum wage laws to tougher crime control. Little of this real advice has ever been quoted, certainly not nearly as much as the fictitious advice.

"Blaming the victim" is another of the mindless clichés of our time. Blame is as irrelevant as bootstraps. No one can be blamed if he did not bring the same skills from Mexico as someone else brought from Germany, or if his school or home did not teach him what people need to know in order to function in a modern technological society. But neither can employers be blamed if people who have more of the required skills are more in demand and others "under-represented." In scientific and technical occupations, for example, Hispanics are under-represented

132

relative to Germans *in Hispanic countries.* Nor is this peculiar. Most of the members of the St. Petersburg Academy of Sciences under the czars were of German ancestry. Chinese students are heavily concentrated in technical fields, from Malaysia to Australia to the United States. People are not magically homogenized by crossing a national border. If anyone should be blamed, it is those who argue as if they are.

# THE IRRELEVANCE OF EVIDENCE

Many who argue most vehemently about race and ethnicity make no distinction whatever between (1) conclusions that follow logically as corollaries from their general vision of society and (2) conclusions for which there is empirical evidence. Indeed, concrete evidence against their conclusions may be countered by *ad hoc* explanations, whose only support is their consonance with the prevailing vision.

Those who support affirmative action, for example, are faced with the embarrassing fact that the economic rise of minorities has slowed noticeably as the "equal opportunity" policies of the 1960s metamorphosed into affirmative action quotas in the early 1970s. An *ad hoc* explanation offered by Christopher Jencks is that "the gains during the 1960s were in 'easy' areas, where resistance was minimal." He adds: "Achieving comparable gains during the 1970s was bound to require stronger pressures on employers."[18] Not a speck of evidence was offered for any aspect of this explanation.

In reality, the historical data show that (1) the economic rise of minorities *preceded* passage of the Civil Rights Act of 1964 by many years, (2) the existing upward trend was *not* accelerated, either by that Act or by quotas that became generally mandatory in 1971, and (3) during the era of affirmative action, such disadvantaged blacks as young males with little experience or education, and members of female-headed households, actually *retrogressed* relative to whites of the same description, while more advantaged blacks rose both absolutely and relative to their white counterparts.[19] In short, although affirmative action invokes the name of the disadvantaged, these are precisely the people who have fallen further behind under its auspices.

Attempts to blame general conditions in the economy or racism among employers run into the hard fact that both advantaged and disadvantaged progress are measured during the same years in the same economy, and one is just as black as the other, especially to racist employers.

These are not mere curious facts. They illustrate effects which elementary economic principles would predict. As the government makes it more dangerous to fire, demote, or even fail to promote, members of minority groups, this tends to increase the demand for the more demonstrably able among them and reduce the demand for the average or below average, or those with too little experience to provide a reassuring track record. But for the true believers in affirmative action, both analysis and evidence are irrelevant.

As in so many other areas of social policy, what matters most politically is not the logic or the facts but the vision —in this case a vision of an incorrigibly corrupt society, whose only saving grace is the presence of a few wise and noble souls, like themselves. Hamlet warned: "Lay not that flattering unction to your soul." But the laying of flattering unction to one's soul has become a major industry, extending far beyond race.

Nor is this a recent development. Back in the late 1960s, Professor Charles L. Black wrote in the *Harvard Law Review* that allowing housing decisions to be made by the marketplace meant "abandoning the Negro to the slum-ghetto that 'private enterprise' has made ready for him."[20] Despite the apparent certitude and air of moral condescension characteristic of those with the civil rights vision, Professor Black advanced no evidence whatever for this conclusion.

In reality, most northern big cities had far less residential segregation of blacks in the late nineteenth century than today, even though (1) there were no "fair housing" laws or policies then, (2) racially restrictive covenants were perfectly legal, (3) blacks had no political power, (4) the federal government took little or no interest in blacks after the Compromise of 1877, and (5) the courts were at best indifferent to blacks during the era from the *Dred Scott* decision of 1857 through *Plessy* v. *Ferguson* in 1896.

In short, all the supposed "prerequisites" for ending rigid ghettoization did not exist—but neither did rigid ghettoization. What changed—dramatically and suddenly —in the early twentieth century were not "perceptions" but realities. The great migrations from the South flooded the northern cities with blacks far less acculturated than those already there—a point made bitterly in the black newspapers of the times and still expressed years later by the "old settlers" in the black community.[21] Rigid segregation in housing developed in this era, in response to this reality. Where the influx from the South occurred earlier—as in Washington, D.C.[22]—the change in racial residential patterns occurred earlier. Where the influx from the South occurred much later—as in San Francisco[23]—the change in racial residential patterns also occurred much later.

"Private enterprise," the supposed villain of the piece, existed both in the early era of wide dispersion of blacks among whites and in the later era of rigid segregation. The striking down of racially restrictive covenants by the Supreme Court in 1948 made no dramatic difference in residential housing patterns. Nor has the rise of government housing projects, free of the taint of private enterprise. As in so many other areas, those with the civil rights vision have made that vision a substitute for evidence.

Nowhere is evidence more irrelevant than when making assertions about the motives of opponents. For example, Professor William Julius Wilson's book, *The Declining Significance of Race,* was explained away in this fashion:

> By writing a book of this nature, Wilson seems bent on being accepted or begging to get into the white academic world because this is what you have to do when you're not in. You're on the periphery . . .

The facts? Wilson is chairman of the department of sociology at the University of Chicago—the top ranked sociology department in the nation. How he could get any more "in" is hard to imagine. A distinguished economist named Joseph A. Schumpeter once pointed out that the only person's motivation we really know is our own—and that what we project onto others provides, at best, clues to our own motives. The man who made this charge against Wilson is a professor of education in an undistinguished university. The charge has, however, been repeated in the media.

A common charge against me is that my own career is due to the very affirmative action I criticize. In all the places where this charge has been repeated, not one bit of evidence has yet been offered. It so happens that I have not achieved anything in my career that was not achieved by other blacks before me—and therefore long before affirmative action.

My graduation from Harvard came more than 80 years

136

after the first black student graduated from Harvard. When I received a Ph.D. from the University of Chicago, it was from an institution that had already produced a disproportionate share of all the black Ph.D.'s in the history of the United States. E. Franklin Frazier was working on his doctorate at Chicago before I was born.

St. Clair Drake asserts that my appointment at Cornell University was "due to black militant pressure"[24]—but without evidence or any apparent sense of need for evidence. When I was offered an appointment at Cornell in December 1964, there weren't enough black students there to pressure anybody to do anything. Blacks were so rare at Cornell that when my wife and I encountered another black couple at a campus restaurant, we all four stopped dead in our tracks, and then burst out laughing.

But even at Cornell, I was not the first black professor of economics. Nor was I the first black economist in the Labor Department or at AT&T, among other places. In all these places I was doing what other blacks had already done—before affirmative action.

The unsupported assertion that my career is due to affirmative action is sometimes accompanied by the unsupported assertion that writing about race has made my career. But in reality I had tenure at U.C.L.A. more than a year before numerical "goals and timetables" were mandated—and before ever publishing a single article or book on race. I had published books on economics and articles in economics journals—as had Abram L. Harris, a black economist a generation before me, who was a full professor at the University of Chicago when I was a graduate student there.

There is no reason why critics should have known such personal trivia. But there is also no reason why they should make sweeping assertions without knowing what they are talking about.

# THE CURRENT CLIMATE

The strong feelings and contending visions that surround issues of race and ethnicity are not enough to explain the current intellectual intolerance and reckless disregard for truth. There have always been strong feelings and contending visions. Yet when W.E.B. Du Bois wrote a highly critical review of a book by his arch rival, Booker T. Washington, he nevertheless referred to Washington's "very evident sincerity of purpose" and acknowledged that he "commands not simply the applause of those who believe in his theories, but the respect of those who do not."[25] We have come a long way since then, but not all of it has been progress.

In the early years of the civil rights movement, there was not only an optimism about the future but a confidence that the facts and rational thinking were on the side of civil rights advocates. *Evidence was an ally.* Chief Justice Earl Warren's portentous reference to "modern authority" in *Brown* v. *Board of Education* symbolized the role of "social science."

One of the many painful contrasts between that era and today is that evidence is increasingly evaded by those who speak in the name of civil rights. Whether it is low test scores or high crime rates, the first order of business is to dismiss the evidence and discredit those who bring it  Even good news—successful minority schools or the rise of a black middle class—is denounced when it does not fit the preconceived vision. Unvarnished facts are today more likely to arouse suspicion and hostility than any joyous anticipation of more ammunition for the good fight.

There are reasons for this. Despite much racial progress, there have also been some very fundamental disappointments. Ghettoes persist, and in many ways are becoming worse for those trapped in them. School integration has largely been thwarted by the demographic facts of "white flight." But even where it has occurred, it has produced neither the educational nor the social miracles once expected. Job barriers have come down but black teenage unemployment has soared to several times what it was 30 years ago. Many white allies in the early struggles for civil rights have become critics of the later phases, such as affirmative action and busing. A small but growing number of black critics has also appeared.

How and why this all happened is a long and complicated story. In essence, however, two things have happened: (1) the battle for civil rights was won, decisively, two decades ago, and (2) the succeeding years have painfully revealed that blatant denials of civil rights were not the universal explanation of social or racial problems. Intellectual and institutional inertia persists in calling racial and ethnic political issues "civil rights" issues and often designing strategy, policies and rhetoric as if they were. Andrew Young perhaps best epitomized this tendency when he said:

> We struggled in the 50s to integrate the schools and the buses. We struggled in the 60s to integrate the lunch counters and the ballot boxes. And we've got to struggle in the 80s to integrate the money.[26]

But the mindset and agenda of the past are no longer working. Like the blind men who each felt only one part of the elephant, many minority leaders mistake that for the whole elephant. Those who point out that other parts are quite different, and that the whole elephant is quite different, are seen as contradicting a tangible reality which has been seized upon and held fast for years. For many, "discrimination" and "racism" are not partial truths but whole truths, not just things to oppose but explanations to cling to, like a security blanket. Evidence that undermines the status of these old enemies also undermines the comforting vision that has grown up around them.

People do not change their vision of the world the way they change clothes or replace old light bulbs. But change they must if they mean to survive. No individual (or group) is going to capture all of reality in his vision. If the only reaction to other visions—or uncomfortable evidence—is blind mudslinging, then the limitations that are common to all human beings become, for them, ideological prisons.

# NOTES

## Chapter 1: The Civil Rights Vision

1. George Gilder, *Wealth and Poverty* (New York: Basic Books, 1980), p. 129.
2. Peter Uhlenberg, "Demographic Correlates of Group Achievement: Contrasting Patterns of Mexican-Americans and Japanese-Americans," *Race, Creed, Color, or National Origin,* ed. Robert K. Yin (Itasca, Illinois: F. E. Peacock Publishers, Inc., 1973), p. 91.
3. Richard A. Easterlin, "Immigration: Economic and Social Characteristics," *Harvard Encyclopedia of American Ethnic Groups,* ed. Stephan Thernstrom, et al. (Cambridge, Mass.: Harvard University Press, 1980), p. 478.
4. Karl E. Taeuber and Alma F. Taeuber, "The Negro Population in the United States," *The American Negro Reference Book,* ed. John P. Davis (Englewood-Cliffs, N.J.: Prentice-Hall, Inc., 1970), p. 112.
5. Jack Chen, *The Chinese of America* (San Francisco: Harper & Row, 1980), p. 18.
6. Yasuo Wakatsuki, "Japanese Emigration to the United States, 1866–1924," *Perspectives in American History,* Vol. XII (1979), pp. 428, 429.
7. *Ibid.,* p. 429.
8. *Ibid.,* p.428.
9. Wolfgang Kollmann and Peter Marschalck, "German Emi-

gration to the United States," *Perspectives in American History,* Vol. VII (1973), pp. 518, 519.

10. George F. W. Young, *The Germans in Chile: Immigration and Colonization, 1849–1914* (New York: Center for Migration Studies, 1974), p. 30.

11. Judith Laikin Elkin, *Jews of the Latin American Republics* (Chapel Hill, N.C.: University of North Carolina Press, 1980), pp. 191, 192.

12. Robert F. Foerster, *The Italian Emigration of Our Times* (New York: Arno Press, 1969), p. 39.

13. Betty Lee Sung, *The Story of the Chinese in America* (New York: Collier Books, 1967), p. 320.

14. Robert E. Kennedy, Jr., *The Irish: Emigration, Marriage, and Fertility* (Berkeley: University of California Press, 1973), p. 78.

15. David S Neft, Roland T. Johnson, Richard M. Cohen, *The Sports Encyclopedia: Baseball* (New York: Grosset & Dunlap, 1976), p. 493.

16. Jeannye Thornton, "Today's Toys—More Than Just Child's Play," *U.S. News and World Report,* December 20, 1982, p. 68.

17. Virginia Thompson and Richard Adloff, *Minority Problems in Southeast Asia* (New York: Russell & Russell, 1955), p. 128.

18. Yuan-li Wu and Chun-hsi Wu, *Economic Development in Southeast Asia* (Stanford: Hoover Institution Press, 1973), p. 22.

19. Robert E. Klitgaard and Ruth Katz, "Ethnic Inequalities and Public Policy: The Case of Malaysia," Mimeographed, Kennedy School of Government, Harvard University, July 1981, p. 11.

20. Thomas Sowell, *The Economics and Politics of Race* (New York: William Morrow, 1983), pp. 80–92.

21. Robert F. Foerster, *The Italian Emigration of Our Times,* p. 262.

22. Thomas Sowell, *Ethnic America* (New York: Basic Books, 1981), pp. 175, 177.

23. U.S. Bureau of the Census, *Historical Statistics of the United States: Colonial Times to 1970* (Washington, D.C.: U.S. Government Printing Office, 1975), p. 422.

24. See *Ibid.*, p. 422; Victor Purcell, *The Chinese in Southeast Asia*, 2nd edition (New York: Oxford University Press, 1980), pp. 406, 514, 519, 527; S. W. Kung, *Chinese in American Life* (Seattle: University of Washington Press, 1962), pp. 14, 15.
25. Carl Degler, *Neither Black Nor White* (New York: Macmillan Publishing Co., 1971), p. 86.
26. Thomas Sowell, "New Light on Black I.Q.," *New York Times Magazine*, March 27, 1977, pp. 57ff; *Idem*, "Race and I.Q. Reconsidered," *Essays and Data on American Ethnic Groups* (Washington, D.C.: The Urban Institute, 1978), pp. 203–238; *Idem.*, "*Weber* and *Bakke* and the Presuppositions of 'Affirmative Action,'" *Wayne Law Review*, July 1980, pp. 1309–1336.
27. *Regents of the University of California* v. *Allan Bakke*, 438 U.S. 265, pp. 365–366.
28. *United Steelworkers of America* v. *Brian F. Weber*, 443 U.S. 193, p. 212n.
29. J. C. Furnas, *The Americans* (New York: G. P. Putnam's Sons, 1969), p. 382.
30. Robert F. Foerster, *The Italian Emigration of Our Times*, pp. 393–394.
31. Kevin O'Connor, *The Irish in Britain* (London: Sidgwick & Jackson, 1972), p. 26.
32. Gary B. Cohen, *The Politics of Ethnic Survival: Germans in Prague, 1861–1914* (Princeton University Press, 1981), p. 126.
33. Nathan Glazer, *Affirmative Discrimination* (New York: Basic Books, 1975), pp. 56–57.
34. Nathan Glazer and Daniel Patrick Moynihan, *Beyond the Melting Pot* (Cambridge, Mass.: M.I.T. Press, 1970), pp. 257–258.
35. Andrew M. Greeley, *That Most Distressful Nation* (Chicago: Quadrangle Press, 1972), p. 129.
36. Kevin O'Connor, *The Irish in Britain*, p. 137.
37. Victor Purcell, *The Chinese in Southeast Asia*, 2nd edition (Kuala Lumpur: Oxford University Press, 1980), p. 107.
38. *Ibid.*

143

39. Lennox A. Mills, *Southeast Asia* (University of Minnesota Press, 1964), pp. 110–111.

40. Victor Purcell, *The Chinese in Southeast Asia*, p. 284.

41. Robert Lacour-Gayet, *A History of South Africa* (New York: Hastings House, 1977), p. 230; W. H. Hutt, *The Economics of the Colour Bar* (London: The Institute of Economic Affairs, 1964), pp. 45–46.

42. Jack Chen, *The Chinese of America* (New York: Harper & Row, 1980), pp. 66–67.

43. Yuan-li Wu and Chun-hsi Wu, *Economic Development in Southeast Asia*, pp. 55–57.

44. Stanford M. Lyman, *Chinese Americans* (New York: Random House, 1974), p. 137.

45. Haitung King and Frances B. Locke, "Chinese in the United States: A Century of Occupational Transition," *International Migration Review*, Vol. 14, M.49 (Spring 1980), p. 22.

46. "In the relatively small number of occupations in which Asians were allowed to participate, they were able to attain a moderate level of economic success." U.S. Commission on Civil Rights, *Unemployment and Underemployment Among Blacks, Hispanics, and Women* (Washington, D.C.: U.S. Commission on Civil Rights, 1982), p. 58. The "deplorable" concentration of Chinese in mathematics, engineering and physics was also considered "evidence of the limited employment opportunities among Chinese intellectuals," in Haitung King and Frances B. Locke, "Chinese in the United States: A Century of Occupational Transition," *International Migration Review*, Vol. 14, No. 49 (Spring 1980), p. 22.

47. J. C. Furnas, *The Americans*, p. 86; Daniel Boorstin, *The Americans* (New York: Random House, 1958), Vol. I, p. 225.

48. Thomas H. Holloway, *Immigrants on the Land* (Chapel Hill, N.C.: University of North Carolina Press, 1980), p. 151; Harry Leonard Sawatsky, *They Sought a Country* (Berkeley: University of California Press, 1971), pp. 129, 244; Arthur Young, *A Tour in Ireland* (Shannon, Ireland: Irish University Press, 1970), Vol. I, pp. 377–379; W. D. Borrie, "Australia," *The Positive Contribution by Immigrants*, ed. Oscar Handlin, et

al. (Paris: United Nations Educational, Scientific and Cultural Organization, 1955), p. 91.

49. Thomas Sowell, *Ethnic America* (New York: Basic Books, 1981), pp. 52–53, 58–59; Emilio Willems, "Brazil," *The Positive Contributions by Immigrants*, ed. Oscar Handlin, et al. (Paris: Unesco, 1955), pp. 122, 130; Charles Wagley, *An Introduction to Brazil* (New York: Columbia University Press, 1971), p. 79; W. D. Borrie, *Italians and Germans in Australia* (Melbourne: The Australian National University, 1934), pp. 93, 94; Gary R. Cohen, *The Politics of Ethnic Survival*, p. 23; Carl Solberg, *Immigration and Nationalism: Argentina and Chile, 1890–1914* (Austin: University of Texas Press, 1970), pp. 41, 101.

50. Theodore Huebner, *The Germans in America* (Radnor, Pa.: Chilton Co., 1962), p. 128; W. D. Borrie, *Italians and Germans in Australia* (Melbourne: The Australian National University, 1934), p. 94; Alfred Dolge, *Pianos and Their Makers* (Covina, Ca.: Covina Publishing Co., 1911), p. 172. Germans apparently were also pioneers in piano manufacturing in Russia. *Ibid.*, p. 264.

51. Emilio Willems, "Brazil," *The Positive Contribution by Immigrants*, ed. Oscar Handlin, et al. (Paris: United Nations Educational, Scientific and Cultural Organization, 1955), p. 133.

52. Solomon Grayzel, *A History of the Jews* (New York: New American Library, 1968), p. 266.

53. Thomas Sowell, *The Economics and Politics of Race*, Chapter 2; David Lowenthal, *West Indian Societies* (New York: Oxford University Press, 1972), pp. 202–208.

54. Naosaku Uchido, *The Overseas Chinese* (Stanford: Hoover Institution Press, 1960), pp. 15–46; Stanford M. Lyman, *Chinese Americans* (New York: Random House, 1974), Chapter 3.

55. Albert Bernhardt Faust, *The German Element in the United States* (New York: Arno Press, 1969), Vol. II, pp. 122–124; Kathleen Neils Conzen, "Germans," *Harvard Encyclopedia of American Ethnic Groups*, ed. Stephan Thernstrom, et al.

(Cambridge, Mass.: Harvard University Press, 1981), p. 421.

56. W. D. Borrie, "Australia," *The Positive Contribution by Immigrants,* ed. Oscar Handlin, pp. 90–94; Emilio Willems, "Brazil," *Ibid.,* pp. 122, 125–128.

57. J. Halcro Ferguson, *Latin America: The Balance of Race Redressed* (London: Oxford University Press, 1961), p. 56.

58. Nathan Glazer and Daniel Patrick Moynihan, *Beyond the Melting Pot,* p. 213.

59. For example, Humberto S. Nelli, *The Italians in Chicago* (New York: Oxford University Press, 1970), pp. 92–100; Herbert J. Gans, *The Urban Villagers* (New York: The Free Press, 1962), p. 174.

60. Robert F. Foerster, *The Italian Emigration of Our Times* (Cambridge, Mass.: Harvard University Press, 1924), Chapters XIII, XIV.

61. Gary B. Cohen, *The Politics of Ethnic Survival: Germans in Prague, 1861–1914* (Princeton: Princeton University Press, 1981), Chapters 1, 2.

62. Alvin Rabushka and Kenneth A. Shepsle, *Politics in Plural Societies: A Theory of Democratic Instability* (Columbus, Ohio: Charles E. Merrill Publishing Co., 1972), pp. 95, 105.

63. *Ibid.,* pp. 122–123.

64. Bernard Lewis, *The Muslim Discovery of Europe* (New York: W. W. Norton & Co., 1982), pp. 24–25, 298.

65. Lynn Hollen Lees, *Exiles of Erin* (Ithaca: Cornell University Press, 1979), p. 223.

66. Raphael Patai, *The Vanished Worlds of Jewry* (New York: Macmillan Publishing Co., Inc., 1980), p. 57.

67. Gary B. Cohen, *The Politics of Ethnic Survival,* pp. 76–83, 175–182, 260–262; Arthur A. Goren, "Jews," *Harvard Encyclopedia of American Ethnic Groups,* p. 576.

68. See, for example, Albert Bernhardt Faust, *The German Element in the United States,* Vol. I, pp. 98–99, 103, 104, 112, 213, 232; Vol. II, p. 423. This is not to claim that Germans had *no* clashes with Indians.

69. *Ibid.,* Vol. I, pp. 45–46, 182, 242, 446.

70. John Hope Franklin, *The Free Negro in North Carolina* (New York: W. W. Norton & Co., 1971), p. 26.
71. Gary B. Cohen, *The Politics of Ethnic Survival*, p. 28.
72. Myron Cohen, *Sons of the Soil: Migration and Ethnic Conflict in India* (Princeton: Princeton University Press, 1978), pp. 285–288; Mary Fainsod Katzenstein, *Ethnicity and Equality: The Shiv Sena Party and Preferential Policies in Bombay* (Ithaca: Cornell University Press, 1979), pp. 72–78.

## *Chapter 2:* From Equal Opportunity to "Affirmative Action"

1. U.S. Equal Employment Opportunity Commission, *Legislative History of Titles VII and XI of Civil Rights Act of 1964* (Washington, D.C.: U.S. Government Printing Office, no date) pp. 1007–08, 1014, 3005, 3006, 3013, 3160, and *passim*.
2. *Ibid.*, p. 3005.
3. *Ibid.*
4. *Ibid.*, p. 1014.
5. *Ibid.*, p. 3006.
6. *Ibid.*, p. 3160.
7. *Ibid.*, p. 3015.
8. *Ibid.*, p. 3013.
9. Quoted in Nathan Glazer, *Affirmative Discrimination* (New York: Basic Books, 1975), p. 45.
10. For example, *Gallup Opinion Index*, Report 143 (June 1977), p. 23.
11. Nathan Glazer, *Affirmative Discrimination*, p. 49.
12. Much semantic effort has gone into claiming that quotas are rigid requirements while "goals" under "affirmative action" are flexible. Historically, however, quotas have existed in sales, immigration, production, and many other areas, sometimes referring to minima, sometimes to maxima, and with varying degrees of flexibility. The idea that "quota" implies rigidity is a recent redefinition. The objection to quotas is that they are quantitative rather than qualitative criteria, not that they are rigidly rather than flexibly quantitative.

13. *United Steelworkers of America* v. *Weber,* 443 US 193 (1979), p. 207, note 7.

14. *Ibid.,* p. 222.

15. *Ibid.,* pp. 226–252.

16. Thomas Sowell, *Markets and Minorities* (New York: Basic Books, 1981), p. 11.

17. U.S. Bureau of the Census, *Social Indicators, 1976* (Washington, D.C.: U.S. Government Printing Office, 1977), pp. 454–456.

18. Peter Uhlenberg, "Demographic Correlates of Group Achievement: Contrasting Patterns of Mexican-Americans and Japanese-Americans," *Race, Creed, Color, or National Origin,* ed. Robert K. Yin (Itasca, Illinois: F. E. Peacock Publishers, 1973), p. 91.

19. Lucy W. Sells, "Leverage for Equal Opportunity Through Mastery of Mathematics," *Women and Minorities in Science,* ed. Sheila M. Humphreys (Boulder, Colorado: Westview Press, 1982), pp. 12, 16.

20. *Ibid.,* p. 11.

21. College Entrance Examination Board, *Profiles, College-Bound Seniors, 1981* (New York: College Entrance Examination Board, 1982), pp. 12, 22, 41, 51, 60, 65.

22. *Ibid.,* pp. 27, 36, 46, 55.

23. *Ibid.,* pp. 60, 79; Alexander Randall, "East Meets West," *Science,* November 1981, p. 72.

24. National Research Council, *Science, Engineering, and Humanities Doctorates in the United States* (Washington, D.C.: National Academy of Sciences, 1980), pp. 13, 39.

25. National Research Council, *Summary Report: 1980 Doctorate Recipients from United States Universities* (Washington, D.C.: National Academy Press, 1981), pp. 26, 29.

26. Sue E. Berryman, "Trends in and Causes of Minority and Female Representation Among Science and Mathematics Doctorates," mimeographed, The Rand Corporation, 1983, p. 13.

27. U.S. Commission on Civil Rights, *Unemployment and Underemployment Among Blacks, Hispanics, and Women* (Washing-

ton, D.C.: U.S. Commission on Civil Rights, 1982), p. 58.

28. Thomas Sowell, *Ethnic America* (New York: Basic Books, 1981), p. 222.

29. J. C. Furnas, *The Americans* (New York: G. P. Putnam's Sons, 1969), p. 86; Daniel Boorstin, *The Americans* (New York: Random House, 1958), Vol. I, p. 225.

30. Arthur Young, *A Tour in Ireland* (Shannon, Ireland: Irish University Press, 1970), Vol. I, pp. 377–379.

31. Thomas H. Holloway, *Immigrants on the Land* (Chapel Hill, N.C.: University of North Carolina Press, 1980), p. 151.

32. Harry Leonard Sawatzky, *They Sought a Country* (Berkeley: University of California Press, 1971), pp. 129, 244. Apparently Germans prospered in Honduras as well. *Ibid.*, pp. 361, 365.

33. Hattie Plum Williams, *The Czar's Germans* (Lincoln, Nebraska: American Historical Society of Germans from Russia, 1975), pp. 135, 159.

34. Carl Solberg, *Immigration and Nationalism* (Austin: University of Texas Press, 1970), pp. 27, 40.

35. Judith Laikin Elkin, *Jews of the Latin American Republics* (Chapel Hill, N.C.: University of North Carolina Press, 1980), pp. 214–237. See also Robert Weisbrot, *The Jews of Argentina* (Philadelphia: The Jewish Publication Society of America, 1979), pp. 175–184.

36. Thomas Sowell, *Ethnic America*, p. 238.

37. Daniel P. Moynihan, "Employment, Income, and the Ordeal of the Negro Family," *Daedalus*, Fall 1965, p. 752.

38. Daniel O. Price, *Changing Characteristics of the Negro Population* (Washington, D.C.: U.S. Government Printing Office, 1969), pp. 117, 118.

39. *Employment and Training Report of the President, 1981* (Washington, D.C.: U.S. Government Printing Office, 1981), p. 150.

40. *Ibid.*, p. 151.

41. Thomas Sowell, *Ethnic America*, p. 260.

42. Thomas Sowell, *The Economics and Politics of Race* (New York· William Morrow, 1983), p. 187.

43. U.S. Bureau of the Census, *Social Indicators III* (Washington, D.C.: U.S. Government Printing Office, 1980), p. 485.

44. Finis Welch, "Affirmative Action and Its Enforcement," *American Economic Review,* May 1981, p. 132.

45. Thomas Sowell, *Affirmative Action Reconsidered* (Washington, D.C.: American Enterprise Institute, 1975), pp. 16–22.

46. Martin Kilson, "Black Social Classes and Intergenerational Policy," *The Public Interest,* Summer 1981, p. 63.

47. U.S. Bureau of the Census *Current Population Reports,* Series P-20, No. 366 (Washington, D.C.: U.S. Government Printing Office, 1981), pp. 182, 184.

48. U.S. Bureau of the Census, *Current Population Reports,* Series P-60, No. 80, p. 37; *Ibid.,* Series P-60, No. 132, pp. 41–42.

49. The probability that a non-discriminatory employer will escape a false charge of discrimination is 95 percent, when the standard of "statistical significance" is that his employment pattern would not occur more than 5 times out of 100 by random chance. But the probability of escaping the same false charge for three separate groups simultaneously is $(.95)^3$ or about 86 percent. When there are six separate groups, the probability is $(.95)^6$ or about 73 percent. Not all groups are separate; women and the aged, for example, overlap racial and ethnic groups. This complicates the calculation without changing the basic principle.

50. The greater ease of "proving" discrimination statistically, when there are multiple groups, multiple jobs, and substantial demographic, cultural and other differences between groups, may either take the form of finding more "discriminators" at a given level of statistical significance (5 percent, for example) or using a more stringent standard of statistical significance (1 percent, for example) to produce a more impressive-looking case against a smaller number of "discriminators."

51. Thomas Sowell, *Affirmative Action Reconsidered* (Washington, D.C.: American Enterprise Institute, 1975), pp. 16–22.

52. Commission on Human Resources, National Research

Council, *Summary Report: 1980 Doctorate Recipients from United States Universities* (National Academy Press, 1981), p. 27.

53. *Ibid.*, p. 25.

54. U.S. Bureau of the Census, *Current Population Reports*, Series P-23, No. 120 (Washington, D.C.: U.S. Government Printing Office, 1982), p. 5.

55. Barry R. Chiswick, "An Analysis of the Earnings and Employment of Asian-American Men," *Journal of Labor Economics*, April 1983, pp. 197–214.

56. Walter McManus, William Gould and Finis Welch, "Earnings of Hispanic Men: The Role of English Language Performance," *Ibid.*, pp. 101–130; Gary D. Sandefur, "Minority Group Status and the Wages of White, Black, and Indian Males," *Social Science Research*, March 1983, pp. 44–68.

## *Chapter 3:* From School Desegration to Busing

1. Richard Kluger, *Simple Justice* (New York: Alfred A. Knopf, 1976), p. 696.

2. *Ibid.*, p. 782.

3. Gloria J. Powell, "School Desegregation: The Psychological, Social, and Educational Implications," *The Psychosocial Development of Minority Group Children*, ed. Gloria J. Powell, p. 439.

4. See, for example, K. B. Clark and M. K. Clark, "The Development of Consciousness of Self and the Emergence of Racial Identification in Negro Pre-School Children," *Journal of Social Psychology*, Vol. 10 (1939), pp. 591–599.

5. Norman Miller, "Changing Views About the Effects of School Desegregation: *Brown* Then and Now," *Scientific Inquiry and the Social Sciences*, ed. Marilynn B. Brewer and Barry E. Collins (San Francisco: Jossey-Bass Publishers, 1981) pp. 413–452.

6. Lino Graglia, *Disaster by Decree* (Ithaca: Cornell University Press, 1976), p. 31.

7. Richard Kluger, *Simple Justice* p. 782.

8. *Ibid.*, p. 720.

9. *Ibid.*, p. 758.
10. Lino Graglia, *Disaster by Decree*, p. 40.
11. *Ibid.*, pp. 38–39.
12. *Ibid.*, p. 48.
13. *Ibid.*, pp. 48–52.
14. *Ibid.*, p. 51.
15. *Ibid.*, p. 66.
16. *Ibid.*, p. 76.
17. *Ibid.*, p. 73.
18. *Ibid.*, Chapter 9.
19. Jack McCurdy, "Egly Makes His Desegregation Order Final," *Los Angeles Times*, July 8, 1980, Part II, pp. 1, 6.
20. Thomas Sowell, "Assumptions versus History in Ethnic Education," *Teachers College Record*, Vol. 83, No. 1 (Fall 1981), pp. 48–51.
21. *Ibid.*, p. 46.
22. *Ibid.*, p. 44.
23. *Ibid.*, pp. 45, 47, 48.
24. Diane Ravitch, *The Great School Wars* (New York: Basic Books, 1974), p. 178.
25. Charles M. Wollenberg, *All Deliberate Speed* (Berkeley: University of California Press, 1978), Chapters 2, 3.
26. *Ibid.*, pp. 73–74; Harry H. L. Kitano, *Japanese Americans* (Englewood Cliffs, N.J.: Prentice-Hall, Inc., 1969), p. 24.
27. "It would take an extraordinarily sophisticated, or perhaps an extraordinarily naive, approach to judicial behavior to believe that the cited literature was the cause of the Court's judgment rather than the result of it." Philip B. Kurland, "Brown v. Board of Education Was the Beginning," *Washington University Law Quarterly*, Vol. 1979, No. 2 (Spring), p. 318.
28. For example, E. Van den Haag, "Social Science Testimony in the Desegregation Cases—A Reply to Professor Kenneth Clark," *Villanova Law Review*, Fall 1960, pp. 69–79; James Gregor, "The Law, Social Science, and School Segregation," *Western Reserve Law Review*. Vol. 14, No. 14, No. 4 (September 1963), pp. 621–636.
29. Richard Kluger, *Simple Justice*, p. 555.

## *Chapter 4:* The Special Case of Blacks

1. James B. Conant, *Slums & Suburbs* (New York: McGraw-Hill, 1961), p. 12.
2. Thomas Sowell, *The Economics and Politics of Race* (New York: William Morrow, 1983), p. 187.
3. U.S. Bureau of the Census, *Statistical Abstract of the United States* (Washington, D.C.: Government Printing Office, 1982), p. 143.
4. Thomas Sowell, *The Economics and Politics of Race*, p. 193.
5. *Ibid.*, p. 103.
6. Audrey M. Shuey, *The Testing of Negro Intelligence*, 2nd edition (New York: Social Science Press, 1966), p. 493.
7. H. J. Eysenck, *The I.Q. Argument* (New York: The Library Press, 1971), p. 23.
8. Phillip E. Vernon, *Intelligence and Cultural Environment* (London: Methuen and Co., Ltd., 1970), p. 155.
9. Lester R. Wheeler, "A Comparative Study of the Intelligence of East Tennessee Mountain Children," *Journal of Educational Psychology*, Vol. 33, No. 5 (May 1942), pp. 322, 324.
10. H. Gordon, *Mental and Scholastic Tests Among Retarded Children* (London: Board of Education Pamphlet No. 44), p. 38.
11. Thomas Sowell, *Race and I.Q. Reconsidered* (Washington, D.C.: The Urban Institute, 1978), pp. 210–211.
12. Herbert G. Gutman, *The Black Family in Slavery and Freedom, 1750–1925* (New York: Vintage Books, 1977), pp. 32, 45.
13. *Ibid.*, p. 455.
14. U.S. Bureau of the Census, *Current Population Reports*, Series P-20, No. 224 (Washington, D.C.: U.S. Government Printing Office, 1971), p. 14.
15. For example, "Thomas Sowell delivers a message to struggling ethnic groups in the United States: Work hard and suffer long." Julia Epstein, "Conservative Advice for Ethnics: Work Hard."
16. Walter E. Williams, *The State Against Blacks* (New York:

McGraw-Hill, 1982), p. 87; Thomas Sowell, *Markets and Minorities* (New York: Basic Books, 1981), pp. 44–46.

17. Thomas Sowell, *Ethnic America* (New York: Basic Books, 1981), Chapter 8.
18. *Ibid.*, pp. 216–220.
19. Thomas Sowell, ed., *Essays and Data on American Ethnic Groups*, p. 258.
20. Thomas Sowell, "Three Black Histories," *Ibid.*, p. 44.
21. Barry R. Chiswick, "The Economic Progress of Immigrants: Some Apparently Universal Patterns," *Contemporary Economic Problems, 1979*, ed. William Fellner (Washington, D.C.: American Enterprise Institute, 1979), p. 373.
22. *Ibid.*, pp. 357–399.
23. Thomas Sowell, *The Economics and Politics of Race.*
24. Richard Freeman, *Black Elite* (New York: McGraw-Hill, 1976), Chapter 4.
25. *Ibid.*, p. 88.
26. U.S. Bureau of the Census, *Current Population Reports*, Series P-20, No. 371 (Washington, D.C.: U.S. Government Printing Office, 1982), p. 7.
27. U.S. Bureau of the Census, *Current Population Reports* Series P-23, No. 80 (Washington, D.C.: U.S. Government Printing Office, no date), p. 44.
28. U.S. Bureau of the Census, *Current Population Reports*, Series P-20, No. 366 (Washington, D.C.: U.S. Govenrment Printing Office, 1981), pp. 182, 184.
29. U.S. Bureau of the Census, *Current Population Reports*, Series P-23, No. 80, p. 44.
30. *Ibid.*, p. 30.
31. James P. Smith and Finis Welch, *Race Differences in Earnings* (Santa Monica, California: The Rand Corporation, 1978), p. 15.
32. Robert Higgs, *Competition and Coercion: Blacks in the American Economy, 1865–1914* (Cambridge: Cambridge University Press, 1977), p. 120.
33. Thomas Sowell, "Patterns of Black Excellence," *The Public Interest*, Spring 1976, pp. 26–58; J. S. Fuerst, "Report from

Chicago: A Program That Works," *Ibid.*, pp. 59–69; Guy D. Garcia, "Hope Stirs in the Ghetto," *Time,* April 25, 1983, p. 95.

34. James S. Coleman, Thomas Hoffer, Sally Kilgore, *High School Achievement* (New York: Basic Books, 1982), pp. 143–145.

35. Thomas Sowell, "Black Excellence: The Case of Dunbar High School," *The Public Interest,* Spring 1974, pp. 1–21.

36. Thomas Sowell, "Patterns of Black Excellence," *op cit.*, pp. 35–37.

37. Thomas Sowell, "Assumptions versus History in Ethnic Education," *Teachers College Record,* Fall 1981, pp. 56–57.

38. Daniel P. Moynihan, "Employment, Income, and the Ordeal of the Negro Family," *Daedalus,* Fall 1965, p. 752.

39. Daniel O. Price, *Changing Characteristics of the Negro Population* (Washington, D.C.: U.S. Government Printing Office, 1969), pp. 118, 133.

40. Orley Ashenfelter, "Changes in Labor Market Discrimination Over Time," *Journal of Human Resources,* Fall 1970, p. 405.

41. David Levering Lewis, *When Harlem Was in Vogue* (New York: Vintage Books, 1982), Chapters 6, 7, *passim.*

42. See, for example, Jacob Mincer, "Unemployment Effects of Minimum Wages," *Journal of Political Economy,* Vol. 84, No. 4, Part 2 (August 1976), p. S103; Walter E. Williams, *Youth and Minority Unemployment* (Stanford: Hoover Institution Press, 1977).

43. U.S. Bureau of the Census, *Current Population Reports,* Series P-60, No. 135 (Washington, D.C.: U.S. Government Printing Office, 1982), p. 3.

44. Walter E. Williams, *The State Against Blacks* (New York: McGraw-Hill, 1982), p. 75.

45. *Ibid.*, pp. 76, 80.
46. *Ibid.*, pp. 85, 86.
47. *Ibid.*, p. 114.
48. *Ibid.*, pp. 113, 114.
49. *Ibid.*, pp. 104–105.
50. *Ibid.*, p. 122.

## Chapter 5: The Special Case of Women

1. Shirley J. Smith, "Estimating Annual Hours of Labor Force Activity," *Monthly Labor Review*, February 1983, p. 15.

2. U.S. Department of Labor, *Employment and Earnings*, Vol. 30, No. 1 (January 1983), p. 169.

3. U.S. Department of Labor, Bureau of Labor Statistics, Bulletin 2162, *Job Tenure and Occupational Change* (Washington, D.C.: U.S. Government Printing Office, 1982), p. 1.

4. U.S. Bureau of the Census, *Current Population Reports*, Series P-60, No. 132 (Washington, D.C.: U.S. Government Printing Office, 1982), p. 161.

5. "The Economic Role of Women," *The Economic Report of the President, 1973* (Washington, D.C.: U.S. Government Printing Office, 1973), p. 103.

6. Helen S. Astin, "Career Profiles of Women Doctorates," *Academic Women on the Move*, eds. Alice S. Rossi and Anne Calderwood (New York: Russell Sage Foundation, 1973), p. 153.

7. Thomas Sowell, *Affirmative Action Reconsidered* (Washington, D.C.: American Enterprise Institute, 1975), pp. 32, 33.

8. William G. Bowen and T. Aldrich Finegan, *The Economics of Labor Force Participation* (Princeton: Princeton University Press, 1969), pp. 40, 41, 97.

9. Shirley J. Smith, "Estimating Annual Hours of Labor Force Activity," *Monthly Labor Review*, February 1983, p. 19.

10. U.S. Bureau of the Census, *Current Population Reports*, Series P-60, No. 132, p. 161.

11. John M. McDowell, "Obsolescence of Knowledge and Career Publication Profiles: Some Evidence of Differences Among Fields in Costs of Interrupted Careers," *American Economic Review*, Vol. 72, No. 4 (September 1982), p. 761.

12. *Ibid.*, p. 757.

13. U.S. Department of Labor, *1975 Handbook on Women Workers* (Washington, D.C.: U.S. Government Printing Office, 1975), p. 28.

14. For example, as a single man I declined a very tempting offer to teach at Dartmouth, because it is located in an

isolated small town, where single living might be socially unattractive. But a year later, as a married man, I accepted a similar offer from Cornell, which is also located in a small isolated town.

15. Thomas Sowell, *Affirmative Action Reconsidered*, pp. 23–24, 30.
16. U.S. Department of Labor, *1975 Handbook on Women Workers*, p. 60.
17. *Ibid.*, p. 20. *See also* Beverly L. Johnson, "Marital and Family Characteristics of the Labor Force," *Monthly Labor Review*, April 1980, p. 51.
18. John B. Parrish, "Professional Womanpower as a National Resource," *Quarterly Review of Economics and Business*, February 1961, p. 58.
19. *Ibid.*, p. 56.
20. Jessie Bernard, *Women and the Public Interest* (Chicago: Aldine Publishing Co., 1971), p. 117.
21. John B. Parrish, "Professional Womanpower as a Soviet Resource," *Quarterly Review of Economics and Business*, August 1964, p. 60.
22. Helen S. Astin, "Career Profiles of Women Doctorates," *Academic Women on the Move*, p. 141.
23. U.S. Bureau of the Census, *Historical Statistics of the United States, Colonial Times to 1970* (Washington, D.C.: U.S. Government Printing Office, 1976), p. 49.
24. Jessie Bernard, *Academic Women* (University Park, Pa.: Pennsylvania State University Press, 1964), pp. 43–44.
25. U.S. Bureau of the Census, *Historical Statistics of the United States, Colonial Times to 1970*, p. 50.
26. U.S. Department of Labor, *1975 Handbook on Women Workers*, p. 28. *See also* William G. Bowen and T. Aldrich Finegan, *The Economics of Labor Force Participation*, p. 88.
27. U.S. Department of Labor, *1975 Handbook on Women Workers*, p. 28.
28. William G. Bowen and T. Aldrich Finegan, *op. cit.*, pp. 89–90, 97.
29. Walter E. Williams, *The State Against Blacks* (New York: McGraw-Hill, 1982), pp. 56, 57.
30. U.S. Bureau of the Census, *Social Indicators III* (Washington, D.C.: U.S. Government Printing Office, 1980), p. 361.

31. *Ibid.*
32. U.S. Department of Labor, *1975 Handbook on Women*, p. 68.
33. Walter E. Williams, *The State Against Blacks*, p. 55.
34. William W. Van Allstyne, "The Proposed Twenty-seventh Amendment: A Brief, Supportive Comment," *Washington University Law Review*, Volume 1979, No. 1 (Winter 1979), p. 203.
35. *Ibid.*, p. 202.
36. Ruth Bader Ginsburg, "Sexual Equality under the Fourteenth and Equal Rights Amendments," *Ibid.*, p. 175.
37. "Panel Discussion," *Ibid.*, p. 206.
38. William W. Van Allstyne, *op. cit.*, p. 203.
39. Ruth Bader Ginsburg, *op. cit.*, p. 161.
40. U.S. Department of Labor, *1975 Handbook on Women*, p. 7.
41. *Ibid.*, p. 28.
42. *Ibid.*, p. iii.
43. Helen S. Astin and Mary Beth Snyder, "Affirmative Action 1972–1982: A Decade of Response," *Change*, July–August 1982, p. 31.
44. *Ibid.*, pp. 28, 29, 30.
45. The Committee on the Status of Women in the Economics Profession reported to the American Economic Association in 1982 that women were "represented more poorly in the top economics departments than they were four years ago"—even though the number of women with Ph.D.'s in economics had doubled. (*The American Economic Review*, May 1983, p. 419.) The top-rated economics departments have long had a pattern of rarely retaining or promoting assistant professors, except for the unusual ones who publish exceptional research. It is a process not unlike panning for gold, where it is understood in advance that only occasional nuggets can be expected. But to hire and then fire large numbers of women without cause—when any one of them could file a costly and time-consuming lawsuit—would be a dangerous gamble under "affirmative action."

46. Tom Jackman, 'Female Professors Gain Little Ground,' *New York Times,* January 9, 1983, Section 3, p. 17.

47  U.S. Commission on Civil Rights, *A Growing Crisis: Disadvantaged Women and Their Children* (Washington, D.C : U.S Commission on Civil Rights, 1983), p. 27.

48. *Ibid.*

49. *Ibid.,* p. 75.

## Chapter 6: Rhetoric or Reality?

1. Yash Tandon, *Problems of a Displaced Minority: The New Position of East Africa's Asians* (London: Minority Rights Group, 1973), p. 15; Yash Ghai and Dharam Ghai, *The Asian Minorities of East and Central Africa* (London: Minority Rights Group, 1979), p. 9.

2. Myron Weiner, *Sons of the Soil: Migration and Ethnic Conflict in India* (Princeton: Princeton University Press, 1978), pp. 285–288. *See also* Mary Fainsod Katzenstein, *Ethnicity and Equality: The Shiv Shena Party and Preferential Policies in Bombay* (Ithaca: Cornell University Press, 1979), Chapter 3.

3. Donald V. Smiley, "French-English Relations in Canada and Consociational Democracy," *Ethnic Conflict in the Western World,* ed. Milton J. Esman (Ithaca: Cornell University Press, 1977), p. 188; Mary Fainsod Katzenstein, *Ethnicity and Equality,* p. 199.

4. Thomas Sowell, *The Economics and Politics of Race: An International Perspective* (New York: William Morrow, 1983), p. 171.

5. Mary Fainsod Katzenstein, *Ethnicity and Equality,* pp. 208–210.

6. Robert Klitgaard and Ruth Katz, "Overcoming Ethnic Inequality: Lessons for Malaysia," *Journal of Policy Analysis and Management,* Vol. 2, No. 3 (1983), pp. 335, 341, 343.

7. *Ibid.,* p. 208.

8. George M. Fredrickson, *White Supremacy: A Comparative Study in American & South African History* (New York: Oxford University Press, 1981), pp. 228–229, 231–233.

9. Robert Higgs, *Competition and Coercion: Blacks in the American*

159

*Economy, 1865–1914* (Cambridge: Cambridge University Press, 1977), pp. 64–66.

10. Robert Higgs, "Landless by Law: Japanese Immigrants in California Agriculture to 1941," *Journal of Economic History,* March 1978, p. 209.

11. Carl Solberg, *Immigration and Nationalism: Argentina and Chile, 1890–1914* (Austin: University of Texas Press, 1970), p. 50; Mark Jefferson, *Peopling the Argentine Pampa* (Port Washington, N.Y.: Kennikat Press, 1971), p. 183; Constance Cronin, *The Sting of Change: Sicilians in Sicily and Australia* (Chicago: University of Chicago Press, 1970), pp. 163, 245; W. D. Borrie, *The Italians and Germans in Australia* (Melbourne: The Australian National University, 1934), p. 147; Luciano J. Iorizzo, "The Padrone and Immigrant Distribution," *The Italian Experience in the United States,* ed. S. M. Tomasi and M. H. Engel (Staten Island, N.Y.: Center for Migration Studies, 1970), p. 57.

12. Dino Cinel, *From Italy to San Francisco: The Immigrant Experience* (Stanford: Stanford University Press, 1982), pp. 237–239; Ronald P. Grossman, *The Italians in America* (Minneapolis: Lerner Publications, 1975), pp. 34–35.

13. Janet Bamford, "Any Port in a Storm," *Forbes,* December 6, 1982, p. 40.

14. Ivan H. Light, *Ethnic Enterprise in America* (Berkeley: University of California Press, 1972), p. 46.

15. Walter E. Williams, "Some Hard Questions on Minority Businesses," *The Negro Educational Review,* April–July 1974, pp. 128–129.

16. Thomas Sowell, *Ethnic America* (New York: Basic Books, 1981), p. 262.

17. *Ibid.,* p. 212.

18. Michael Meltsner, *Cruel and Unusual: The Supreme Court and Capital Punishment* (New York: Random House, 1973), p. 36.

19. Luigi Barzini, *The Europeans* (New York: Simon & Schuster, 1983), p. 106.

20. For example, *Gallup Opinion Index,* June 1977, Report 143, p. 23.

# Epilogue

1. Thomas Sowell, "New Light on Black IQ," *New York Times Magazine*, March 27, 1977, pp. 57 ff; Thomas Sowell, "Race and IQ Reconsidered," *Essays and Data on American Ethnic Groups* (Washington: The Urban Institute, 1978), pp. 203–238; Thomas Sowell, *Black Education: Myths and Tragedies* (New York: David McKay Co., 1972), pp. 265–295; Thomas Sowell, "The Great IQ Controversy," *Change*, May 1973, pp. 33–37; Thomas Sowell, *Knowledge and Decisions* (New York: Basic Books, Inc., 1980), pp. 345–349; Thomas Sowell, *Ethnic America* (New York: Basic Books, Inc., 1981), pp. 281–282.

2. CBS Correspondent Lem Tucker declared on the *CBS Morning News* broadcast of October 13, 1981, that my position "seems to place him in the school that believes that maybe most blacks are genetically inferior to whites." A similar innuendo appeared in William Darity, Jr., "The Goal of Racial Economic Equality," *The Journal of Ethnic Studies*, Winter 1983, p. 54.

3. Tom Braden, "Economist's Message Is Wrong," Mount Prospect, Illinois, *Daily Herald*, January 2, 1983.

4. Christopher Jencks, "Discrimination and Thomas Sowell," *New York Review of Books*, March 3, 1983, p. 33.

5. Carl Rowan, "What Has Reagan Learned About U.S. Blacks?" *Los Angeles Herald-Examiner*, December 27, 1980, p. A13.

6. Thomas Sowell, *Black Education: Myths and Tragedies*, p. 111.

7. *CBS Morning News*, broadcast of October 13, 1981.

8. Lester Thurow, *The New Republic*, June 28, 1980, p. 900.

9. Christopher Jencks, *op. cit.*, p. 37.

10. Patricia Roberts Harris, "Who Speaks for Black People?" *The Washington Post*, February 18, 1981.

11. Roger Wilkins, "Sowell Brother?" *The Nation*, October 10, 1981, p. 332.

12. St. Clair Drake, "The Value of Cultural Baggage," *Palo Alto Weekly*, September 23, 1981, p. 1.

13. Christopher Jencks, *op. cit.*, p. 34.
14. U.S. Commission on Civil Rights, *Unemployment and Underemployment Among Blacks, Hispanics, and Women* (Washington: U.S. Commission on Civil Rights, 1982), p. 40.
15. See Chapter 2 above.
16. Christopher Jencks, *op. cit.*, p. 34.
17. U.S. Commission on Civil Rights, *op. cit.*, p. 58.
18. Christopher Jencks, "Ethnic America: An Exchange," *New York Review of Books*, June 16, 1983, p. 50.
19. See Chapter 2 above.
20. Charles L. Black, "Foreword: 'State Action,' Equal Protection and California's Proposition 14," *Harvard Law Review*, Vol. 81, No. 69 (1967), p. 109.
21. Allan H. Spear, *Black Chicago* (Chicago: University of Chicago Press, 1970), p. 168; E. Franklin Frazier, *The Negro in the United States* (New York: The Macmillan Co., 1971), pp. 284–285; Florette Henri, *Black Migration: Movement North, 1900–1920* (New York: Anchor Books, 1976), pp. 96–97, Gilbert Osofsky, *Harlem: The Making of a Ghetto* (New York: Harper and Row, 1966), p. 44; Ivan H. Light, *Ethnic Enterprise in America* (Berkeley: University of California Press, 1972), Figure 1 (after p. 100).
22. Constance M. Green, *The Secret City* (Princeton: Princeton University Press, 1967), p. 127.
23. Douglas Henry Daniels, *Pioneer Urbanites* (Philadelphia: Temple University Press, 1980), Chapter 10.
24. St. Clair Drake, "The Value of Cultural Baggage," *The Palo Alto Weekly*, September 23, 1981, p. 1.
25. W.E.B. Du Bois, *Book Reviews by W.E.B. Du Bois*, ed. Herbert Aptheker (Millwood, N.Y.: KTO Press, 1977), p. 5.
26. Quoted in William Darity, Jr., *op. cit.*, p. 51.

# INDEX

163

*Also available from Quill*

**The Economics and Politics of Race:
An International Perspective**
Thomas Sowell

Renowned economist Thomas Sowell uses
hard facts to demonstrate that internationally as well as domestically, discrimination, however heinous, is not a cause of
poverty.

0-688-04832-3

*At your local bookstore*